MathsBeat

CW01653648

Year 2
Teacher's Handbook

Mike Askew
Robert Wilne
Rachel Rayner
Rebecca Hamburger
Janine Blinko

OXFORD
UNIVERSITY PRESS

OXFORD
UNIVERSITY PRESS

Great Clarendon Street, Oxford, OX2 6DP, United Kingdom

Oxford University Press is a department of the University of Oxford. It furthers the University's objective of excellence in research, scholarship, and education by publishing worldwide. Oxford is a registered trade mark of Oxford University Press in the UK and in certain other countries

First published in 2019

British Library Cataloguing in Publication Data
Data available

9780198435587

10 9 8 7 6 5 4 3 2 1

Paper used in the production of this book is a natural, recyclable product made from wood grown in sustainable forests. The manufacturing process conforms to the environmental regulations of the country of origin.

Printed in Great Britain by Ashford Colour Press

Acknowledgements
Written and developed by Mike Askew, Robert Wilne, Rachel Rayner, Rebecca Hamburger, Janine Blinko

Cover illustrations: vectoriart/iStockphoto

Photographs by Emma Lowndes, except: pages 28, 39, 40, 41, 42, 43, 104, 105, 106 and 107 by Earl Smith

With special thanks to: Bickley Primary School, Bromley; Deer Park School, Richmond-upon-Thames; Halley House School, London; Oaks Primary Academy, Kent; Pickhurst Infant Academy, West Wickham; St Lawrence CE Primary School, Alton; Sundridge and Brasted C of E Primary School, Sundridge.

MathsBeat Year 2 Teacher's Handbook

Contents

MathsBeat Year 2 Teacher's Handbook

MathsBeat is a digitally-led resource to support teaching for mastery, crafted by teachers who understand the challenges of teaching within a UK classroom. At the heart of *MathsBeat* is the desire to make maths more available to more children. This has driven the way we've developed the *MathsBeat* materials and our thinking about the teaching sequence.

Two principles have been used throughout the programme:

1. Mathematical thinking is a natural human ability that all children can do by solving problems. Through learning maths, we can teach children to find the most efficient ways to solve problems.
2. No two classrooms are the same. *MathsBeat* provides progression with built-in flexibility and regular formative assessment support, so teachers can choose to spend longer on a task or decide that their children are ready to move on. By using the sequences of carefully designed learning tasks, children will develop knowledge, fluency, reasoning and understanding.

As part of our development work, we asked our community of teachers to trial tasks from the *MathsBeat* Digital Planner. Their experiences informed developments to the tasks themselves and were also collated to form this professional development handbook based on real classroom experience.

One of the unique features of *MathsBeat* is that it's designed to be used in a structured yet flexible way. This handbook aims to encourage that flexibility. Importantly, when trialling tasks in classrooms within our teaching community, we captured children's misconceptions and teachers' responses, resulting in the wealth of coaching support provided in the handbook. So while it has progression and formative assessment built in, *MathsBeat* importantly recognizes that only teachers can decide when their children need to spend a bit longer working on something and when they are ready to move onto the next task. In this way, every child can be at the heart of learning maths and develop the depth of learning they need.

Acknowledgements

We would like to thank all the teachers and children who have trialled our tasks, given us feedback and contributed to ideas and suggestions. Special thanks go to Bickley Primary School, Bromley; Deer Park School, Richmond-upon-Thames; Halley House School, London; Oaks Primary Academy, Kent; Pickhurst Infant Academy, West Wickham; St Lawrence CE Primary School, Alton; Sundridge and Brasted C of E Primary School, Sundridge.

About the Series Editors

Mike Askew is an internationally renowned expert in Primary mathematics education who believes that all children can act as mathematicians, given rich, engaging and challenging problems to reason about. He has taught at all levels, including teacher professional development, and led research projects throughout the world. He now researches, speaks and writes about teaching and learning mathematics. Mike believes that all children can find mathematical activity engaging and enjoyable and therefore develop the confidence in their ability to do maths.

Robert Wilne co-led the initial National Centre for Excellence in the Teaching of Mathematics (NCETM) England-Shanghai teacher exchanges, supporting Maths Hubs as they introduced teaching for mastery. He has over 20 years' experience teaching primary and secondary maths and works regularly in schools coaching and training maths teachers and developing curriculum resources.

Our teaching community

MathsBeat has been created alongside a community of teachers who have been involved at every stage of development. These teachers bring with them experience of a variety of different school types, from 3-form entry, inner-city schools to small rural schools with mixed-aged classes and from 2% to 80% English as an Additional Language (EAL). The teachers range from newly-qualified teachers to established practitioners, from classroom teachers to subject leaders, and have a variety of experience of maths mastery, to ensure that our teacher community reflects the diversity of classrooms across the United Kingdom.

At each stage, their feedback has led us to evolve the content to make sure it is fit for purpose and has an impact in schools. Through this trialling of content in classrooms across the country, we collated the authentic photographs and conversations that form this handbook.

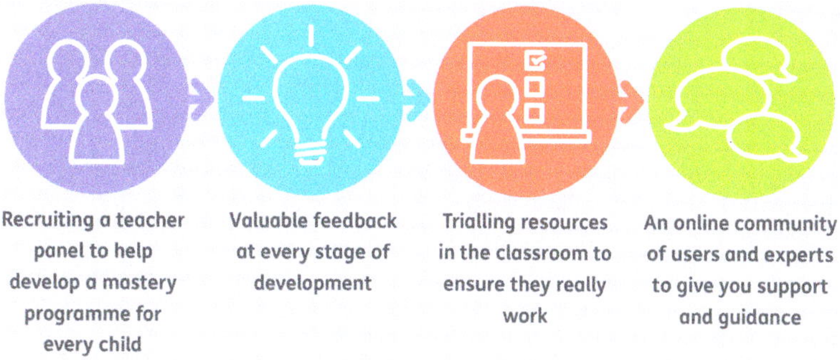

Our teaching community can be found on Facebook, where you can go to for practical tips and advice from your peers, as well as the expert author team.

Chapter 1
Number and place value

Strand overview

Aims

Children reason about how the position (place) of a digit in a number determines its value. They solve problems by translating word problems into pictorial representations, e.g. bar models, as a way of establishing the relationship between quantities. They develop fluency in counting in ones, twos, threes, fives and tens.

Key ideas

- Children appreciate that in a 2-digit number, the tens digit is the 'big picture' and the ones digit is the 'fine detail'. This helps avoid the misconception that the values of digits in a numeral determine its magnitude, e.g. 39 must be bigger than 42 because 9 is a 'big' number.
- Each counting number (positive integer) can be placed in a unique position on a number line, and the distance between any two consecutive counting numbers on a particular number line is always the same.
- Children accurately estimating where to position a number on a partially-labelled number line has been shown to be a predictor of later success in number.
- Children need to become familiar with two meanings of zero. First, that zero is the answer when you count a group with no objects in it, and second that zero can be used as a placeholder, and has meaning when used, e.g. 'no tens' is not 'nothing at all'; it conveys information about the number.
- Developing a sound understanding of place value involves using it to effectively enumerate (establish the total in) large quantities of items, not simply attending to digits on the page.

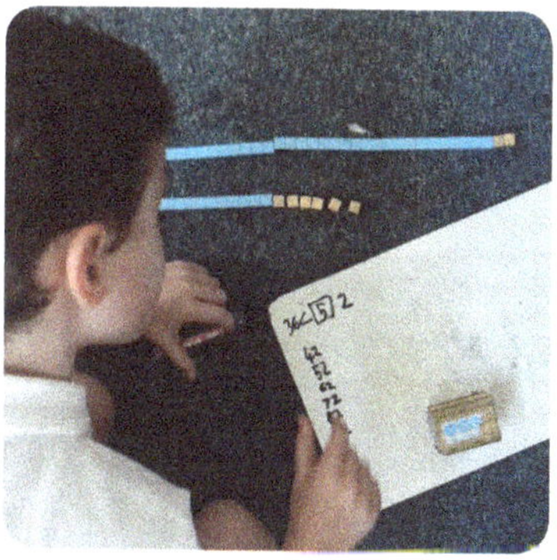

Models and apparatus

Children should work with a wide variety of representations, including collections of real objects, 10-frames, base-ten apparatus, £1, 10p and 1p coins, number tracks, 100-squares and number lines. An unmarked counting stick helps to develop fluency in skip counting forwards and backwards. Working with partially labelled number lines, e.g. only multiples of 5 or 10 marked, helps prepare children to work with the empty number line.

View the video on the Year 2 Teacher Support area of the Digital Planner

Progression through the National Curriculum

Year 1

- Count to and across 100, forwards and backwards, beginning with 0 or 1, or from any given number.
- Count, read and write numbers to 100 in numerals; count in multiples of twos, fives and tens.
- Given a number, identify one more and one less.
- Identify and represent numbers using objects and pictorial representations including the number line, and use the language of: equal to, more than, less than (fewer).
- Read and write numbers from 1 to 20 in numerals and words.

Year 2

- Count in steps of 2, 3 and 5 from 0, and in tens from any number, forward and backward.
- Recognize the place value of each digit in a 2-digit number (tens, ones).
- Identify, represent and estimate numbers using different representations, including the number line.
- Compare and order numbers from 0 up to 100; use <, > and = signs.
- Read and write numbers to at least 100 in numerals and in words.
- Use place value and number facts to solve problems.

Year 3

- Count from 0 in multiples of 4, 8, 50 and 100; find 10 or 100 more or less than a given number.
- Recognize the place value of each digit in a 3-digit number (hundreds, tens, ones).
- Compare and order numbers up to 1000.
- Identify, represent and estimate numbers using different representations.
- Read and write numbers up to 1000 in numerals and in words.
- Solve number problems and practical problems involving these ideas.

Year 2 sub-objectives

Term 1

- Count in steps of 2, 3 and 5 from 0, and in tens from any number, forward and backward.
- Recognize the place value of each digit in a 2-digit number (tens, ones).
- Identify, represent and estimate numbers using different representations, including the number line.
- Read and write numbers to at least 100 in numerals and in words.

Term 2

- Use place value and number facts to solve problems.

Term 3

- Identify, represent and estimate numbers using different representations, including the number line.
- Compare numbers from 0 up to 100, using <, > and = signs.
- Compare and order numbers from 0 up to 100, using <, > and = signs.

Tasks in Practice

Learning task 1: Show me the number

DP Year 2 > Term 1 > Unit 1 > Number and place value > Week 2 > Learning task 1

In this task, children represent 2-digit numbers using a range of representations.

On track

Children who are 'on track' make connections between a range of representations for a given number. They identify a number represented using concrete apparatus, and also use a range of resources to represent a particular number.

Children were asked to represent the number 57 in different ways.

T: Can you explain what you've done, Alex?

C1: *I've done a bar model for fifty-seven and it stands for fifty-seven. And I've done a part-part-whole model with fifty-seven and fifty and seven. And I've done lines with fives and seven because there's five tens and seven ones. And I've done five tens in place value counters and I've done seven ones in counters. And I've shown five tens and seven ones. And I've done place value cards: two twenties and one ten and seven ones.*

How does the bar model show 57? Children need to identify that the whole is 57.

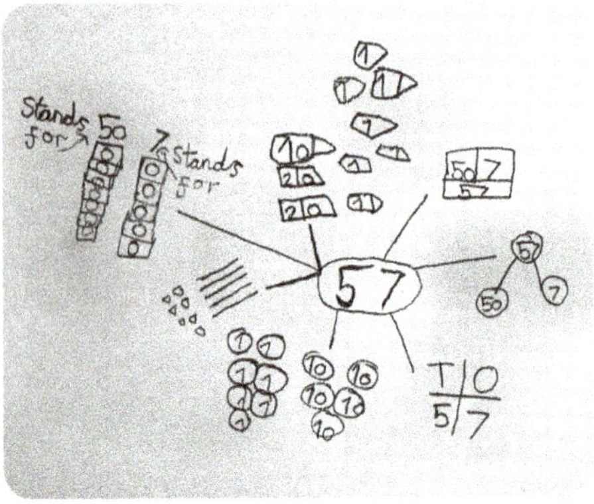

◄ Look again at your cubes. Have you shown the right number of tens and ones in your drawing?

T: Have you done anything different, Malia?

C2: Yes, I did it with 10-frames, five full and one with seven in. And I drew a bead string with fifty-seven beads. And I wrote calculations: fifty add seven equals fifty-seven, seven add fifty equals fifty-seven, and fifty-eight take away one equals fifty-seven.

If a child has begun to represent the number in single ones (e.g. with counters or by drawing single dots), bring them back by asking them to represent their ideas using place value apparatus.

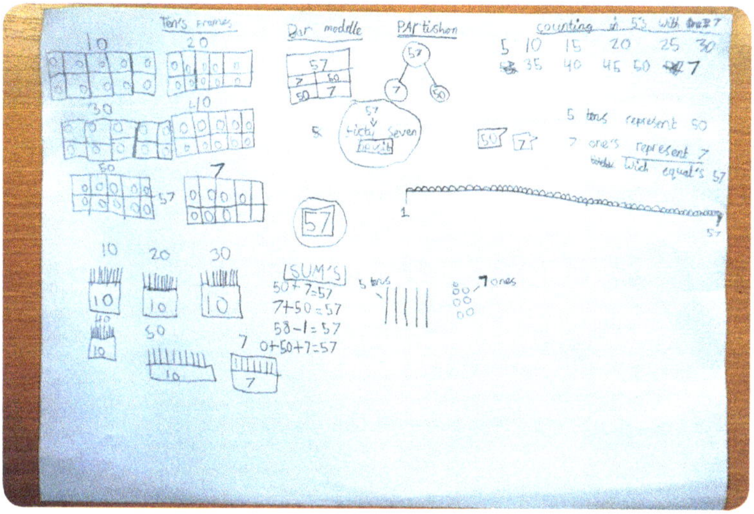

▲ Different representations of the number 57.

Ask children which representations they find clearest and why.

What next?

Provide children with three different representations of the same number including one deliberate non-example. Ask children to find which one could be the odd one out and explain why.

Ask: *Which one could be the odd one out?* This encourages children to think of more than one answer, and to reason.

Needing support

Look and listen for children not identifying that, e.g. 3 tens and 4 ones using base-ten apparatus is the same as 3 full 10-frames with 4 counters remaining.

Example 1

This child has drawn representations of the number 24.

T: I like how you're partitioning that. Tell me about what you're doing.

C: I did a part-part-whole model.

T: Nice. What else have you done?

C: I've done a 10-frame.

T: Tell me about your 10-frames.

C: I did twenty here, because the tens is twenty, and then I did four cubes here.

How did you know that you needed 2 tens to make 20?

T: You can tell me if I'm wrong, but I'm counting two, four, six, eight ones. But here (teacher points to the part-part-whole model), you told me there are four ones. So I'm a bit confused. Can you help me?

C: Well let's cross those out so there are only four left.

T: OK, but why do you only need four?

C: Because the whole is twenty-four so you only need four ones. Because if you had eight then it would be twenty-eight.

T: Great reasoning. Can you change that for me?

(Child crosses out the 4 additional ones.)

The teacher's feedback is showing that they value the explanation as well as the numerical answer.

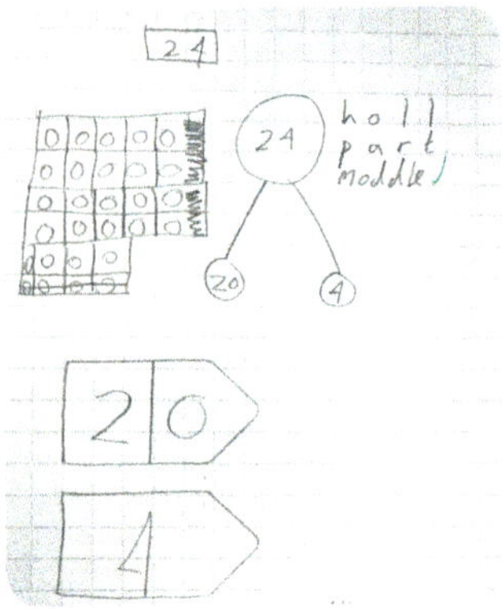

◀ Representations of 24. The 10-frames on the left showed 28 but the child crosses out 4 ones to show 24.

Example 2

This child has difficulty distinguishing between tens and ones. The teacher supports using base-ten apparatus, and links to 10-frames.

T: How many tens have you got?

C: Two.

T: Amazing, and how many ones have you got?

C: Two.

T: So how much have you got altogether?

C: Two.

T: Altogether?

C: One, two, three, four.

T: Well we've got four things to count, haven't we, but if that means ten (teacher points to a 10-rod), you've got ten ...

C: Ten, twenty, thirty ...

T: Is that ten?

(Teacher points at a 1-cube.)

C: Mmm ...

T: That's not ten! What does that mean?

C: One.

T: One! So what do we have then?

C: Ten, twenty here.

T: Good!

C: One, two here.

T: And what is that altogether?

C: Twenty-one, twenty-two.

T: Right!

The teacher uses 10-rods to help the child distinguish between the tens and ones.

▲ This child creates representations for 22 with support.

What next?

Create groups of counters for numbers up to 30. Place the counters onto 10-frames to show how each number is grouped into tens and ones. For each number, ask children how many complete 10-frames were made and how many counters were in the incomplete frame.

Also show an 'incorrect' frame (e.g. three frames but not all full, or some overfull), and two counters in a fourth frame, and claim that it represents 32. Do children agree?

'Non-examples' are very helpful in determining what children securely understand.

Going deeper

Ask children to match different representations of the same number. Ask them which might be the odd one out of a selection of representations.

The teacher shows children a number of hand-drawn representations for 37. She uses place value cards, the word 'Thirty-six', the numerals 37, place value counters, 37 represented as a part-part-whole model (labelled 37, 3, 7) and 37 shown with base-10 apparatus.

T: I have represented a number in six ways. I want you to tell me what the odd one out could be and why you think so.

(Child counts the ones in the tens and ones counters drawing.)

C: *One, two, three, four, five, six, seven. It's definitely that one.*

(Child points to 'Thirty-six'.)

T: Why?

C: *Because it doesn't have seven.*

T: What do you mean? What's my number?

C: *Thirty-seven.*

T: OK.

C: *And thirty-six is the odd one out.*

T: Why is thirty-six the odd one out?

C: *Because it's got a six for its ones instead of a seven.*

T: Good reasoning. Is there another odd one out?

C: *That's the only one in words.*

T: It's the only one in words, OK. Anything else that could be the odd one out? Have I made any mistakes? Ooh, why are you pointing at my three?

(Child points to part-part-whole model with the two parts shown as 3 and 7.)

C: *Because I know the whole is thirty-seven but I thought three and seven equals ten.*

T: OK, but I told you I partitioned thirty-seven into three and seven. Is that not right?

C: *No, because it needs to be thirty and seven.*

The openness of this initial instruction allows the teacher to determine what children 'see' in the representations.

*Remember, it is the value of the number that is important. We are looking for the one that is not the same **value** as the others.*

The teacher gently pushes the child to explain the choice, rather than just state it.

T: Can you correct that? What do I need to write in here, what's my number?

C: *You need to change three to thirty.*

T: Is there any other way I could represent thirty-seven?

C: *Yes, I think a bar model.*

(Child draws a bar model.)

▲ Child adds a bar model for 37 to the teacher's 'odd-one out' representation.

T: Can you label that diagram so I know exactly what you mean?

(Child labels the diagram 3 tens and 7 ones.)

How could you ask children to relate the part-part-whole to the bar model?

What next?

Ask children to create their own odd one out examples for their partner to find.

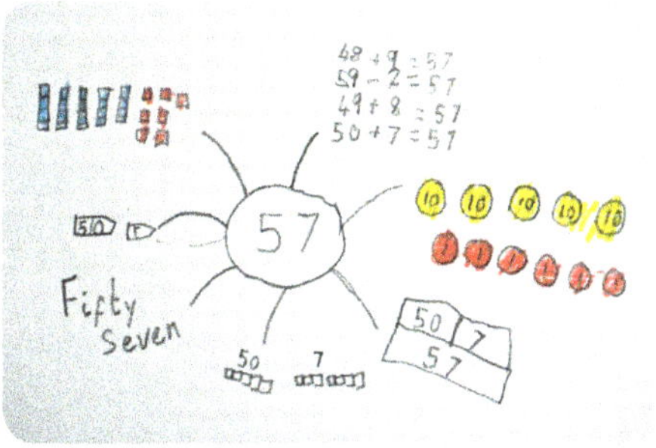

◀ This child has made an 'odd one out' problem for 57, by adding only 6 red 1-counters to their drawing.

Tasks in Practice

Learning task 3: What is the problem?

DP Year 2 > Term 2 > Unit 7 > Number and place value > Week 1 > Learning task 3

In this task, children create word problems to match a given visual representation.

On track

Children who are 'on track' identify the additive structure represented pictorially and translate this to form a word problem of their own creation.

Children have been shown an image of four 10-frames; the first three are full of counters, and the fourth contains six counters. Children have been asked to construct a word problem related to the image.

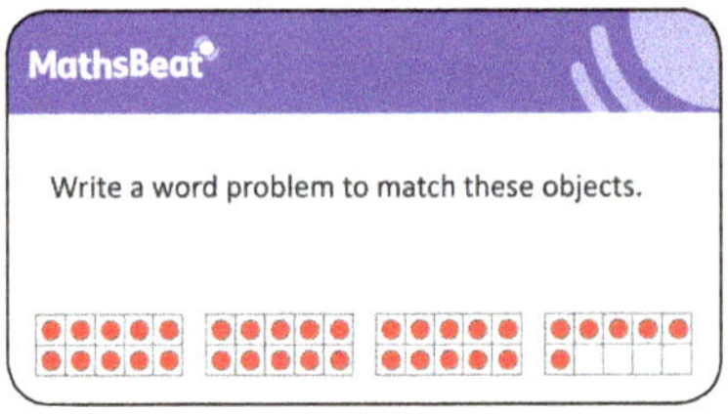

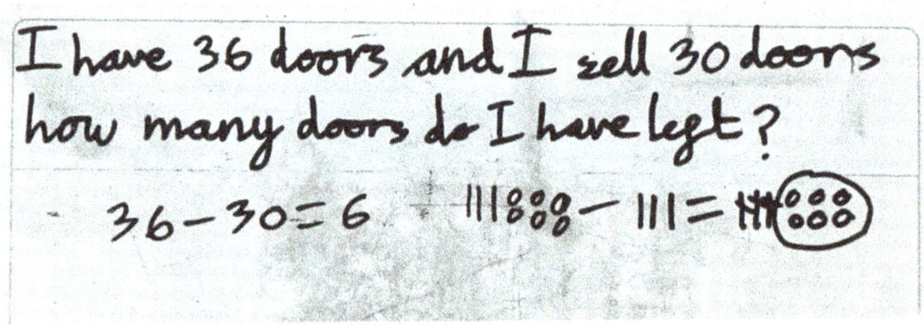

▲ A child's word problem: I have 36 doors and I sell 30 doors. How many doors do I have left? 36 − 30 = 6.

C: *I have thirty-six doors and I sell thirty doors. How many doors will I have left?*

T: Nice, you've written a subtraction. What was your start number?

How is the representation using the 10-frame supporting the concept of place value here?

C: *Thirty-six.*

T: Thirty-six. And what was the change?

C: *Take away thirty.*

T: So the change was take away because you sold thirty doors. You started with thirty-six. You say the change was take away thirty. What was the result?

C: *Six.*

T: Yes, six, because you had six doors left. Write me two more of your door problems using thirty-six as your start number but changing the other numbers.

Asking for more than one example is a good way of drawing out the extent of children's understanding.

What's the same and what is different about this problem?

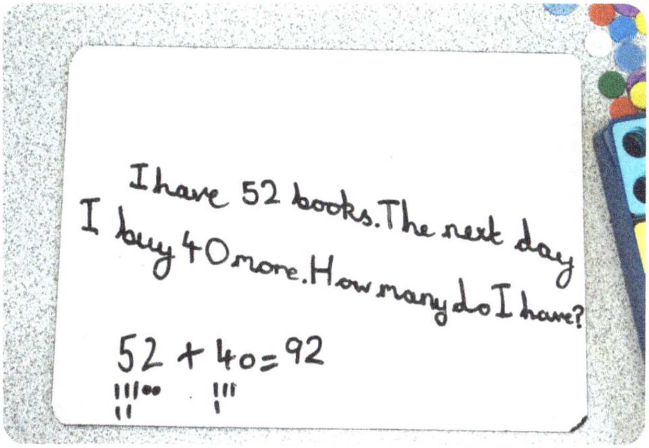

▲ Children were shown a second image: 52 cubes (5 tens and 2 ones), followed by 40 cubes (4 tens). They were asked to write a word problem to fit the image.

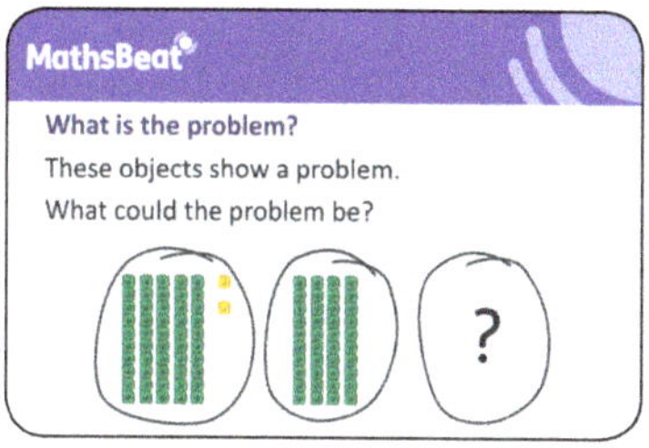

What next?

Children work in pairs. One child makes a representation pictorially and their partner writes a word problem for it.

Needing support

Look and listen for children not translating an image into a related word problem. Children may make errors such as number of items or position of the unknown in the problem.

Child 2 has drawn an image of base-ten apparatus: 3 tens and 6 ones, followed by 4 tens. Child 1 is writing a word problem to match.

▲ Child 1's word problem: 36 − 40 = □
36 marbles I give 40 away.

T: What are the numbers you're using?

C1: Thirty-six and forty.

T: Can you tell me about the word problem you've written?

C1: I have thirty-six marbles. I give forty away.

T: OK, so you started with thirty-six marbles. And the thing you're changing is to give away forty of them?

C1: Yes.

T: So what's the result? How many marbles do you have now?

C2: Four.

T: Are you sure about that? Let's try it with base-ten apparatus. Can you show me thirty-six?

(Children place three 10-rods and six 1-cubes together on an individual whiteboard. Teacher writes 36 below them.)

This child is correctly seeing the difference between 36 and 40 but not applying the part-part-whole relationship securely.

T: What do you need to do next?

C1: Take away forty.

T: OK, give it a try.

(Child 1 starts removing the apparatus and then puts it back.)

C1: I can't take away forty. There aren't enough.

T: That's right, forty is more than thirty-six. Maybe we need to change the story a bit. What if forty was the result, not the change? So forty is the number of marbles you have at the end?

(Teacher places four 10-rods on the right-hand side of the whiteboard and writes 40 below them.)

T: How many would we need to add on to thirty-six to get to forty?

C2: Four.

(Teacher places four 1-cubes in the middle of the whiteboard and writes 4 below it. She writes + and = between the three sets of apparatus.)

T: Can you tell me a story about marbles to match this addition sentence?

C1: I had thirty-six marbles. I got four more. Then I had forty.

The teacher's encouraging language helps the child to come to the realization by themselves, without feeling they've 'got it wrong'.

How could we rearrange the numbers in your number sentence so that the result was still four?

The child's confusion is with subtraction. Is moving to addition here supporting this?

What next?

Show children a concrete representation, using smaller numbers. Guide them through the process of constructing a suitable word problem, emphasizing the start, change and result. Give particular focus to examples of subtraction.

Going deeper

Ask children to create three word problems to fit a given visual representation, labelling the parts that are the start, change and result.

T: I want you to choose one of these representations, and write three different word problems for it.

(Child chooses an image showing 30 on one bead string and 37 on another bead string.)

C: *One, two, three, four, five, six, seven* (child counts the ones beads). *So it's sixty-seven.*

T: So you've put them together. What could your first word problem be?

C: *I have sixty-seven pencils.*

T: Then what are you going to do?

C: *Take away thirty.*

T: So how are you going to put it in a sentence?

(Child writes: I have 67 pencils. I use 30 pencils. How many do I have now?)

T: Can you write the number sentence?

C: *Sixty-seven take away thirty equals thirty-seven.*

(Child writes: 67 – 30 = 37.)

T: What's your start number?

C: *Sixty-seven.*

T: Can you write that for me?

(Child writes 'start' above 67.)

T: And what are the other parts?

C: *The change is take away thirty.*

(Child writes 'change' under 30.)

T: And what is thirty-seven in your number sentence?

C: *The result!*

(Child writes 'result' above 37.)

T: Good. You've got two more to do. I'll come back and see them in a bit.

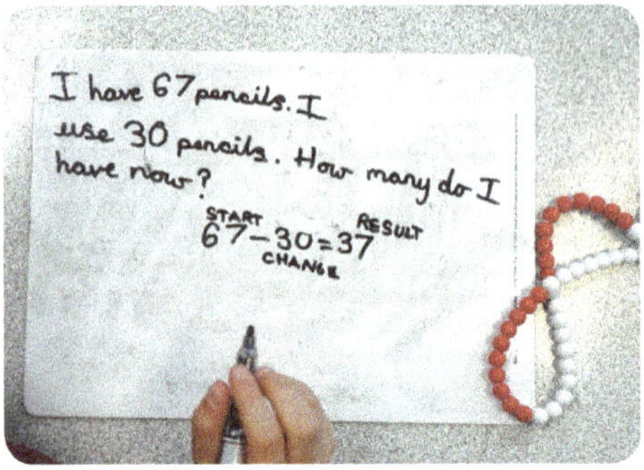

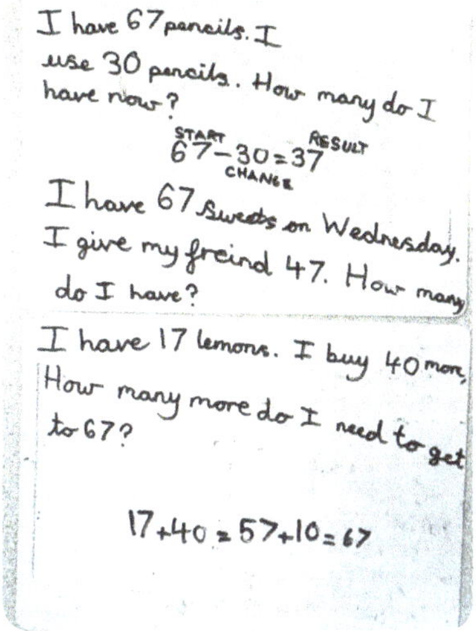

◀ This child varies the problem numbers but keeps the structure the same.

The child has used the same structure but different numbers. How could you ensure children use the same numbers but vary the structure?

How would you draw out from the child a correct expression of their thinking?

T: You've got some really lovely word problems here! Now I want you to see if you can come up with three **different** sentences that use the **same** three numbers. Thirty, thirty-seven and sixty-seven.

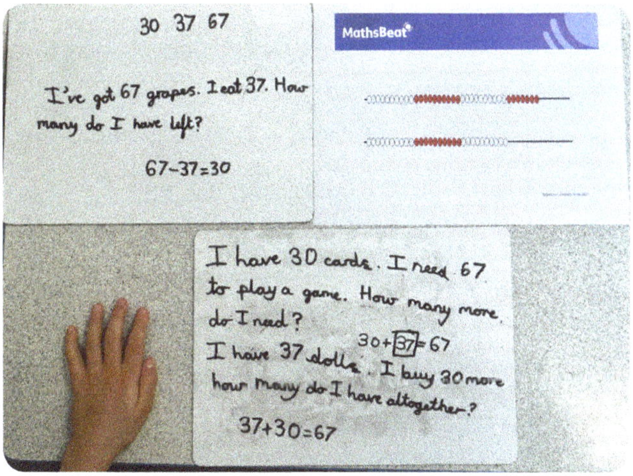

▲ This child keeps the numbers the same and successfully varies the problem structure.

What next?

Ask children how many different ways they could create word problems using the same three numbers. Remind them to think about addition, subtraction, and which of the three numbers is the unknown.

Tasks in Practice

Learning task 2: Making statements true

DP Year 2 > Term 3 > Unit 14 > Number and place value > Week 1 > Learning task 2

In this task, children complete missing-number statements to make < = > statements true.

On track

Children who are 'on track' complete number statements and justify their choice of symbol or digit using place value apparatus.

Example 1

This child has been exploring possibilities for 1 □ > 14.

T: How did you decide which number to start with?

C: *I started by adding one to fourteen to get fifteen.*

T: Why did you do that?

C: *It's only one more than fourteen, so that must be the smallest the answer could be.*

T: How did you find all the possibilities?

C: *I just kept adding one: sixteen, seventeen, eighteen, nineteen.*

T: Is that all the possibilities?

C: *Yes, because it has to work with this empty box. Twenty is bigger than fourteen but that won't work because I only have one ten, and twenty has two tens.*

T: What numbers can't it be?

C: *Ten, eleven, twelve and thirteen. And fourteen.*

T: Why is that?

C: *They're all smaller. And fourteen is the same.*

How could you emphasize the importance of reading the statement from left to right when reasoning about the numbers in a given statement?

How could a number line be helpful here?

Example 2

The teacher shows 56 > □ 2.

T: Could I put any digit in here?

C: No.

T: Can you write down some possibilities?

(Children work in pairs.)

T: Show me your boards. Brilliant, you've worked systematically. What did you put first?

C: Twelve.

T: Good, fifty-six is greater than twelve. What next? Fifty-six is greater than ...

C: Twenty-two.

T: And then ...

C: Thirty-two.

T: Good. When did you stop?

C: When I'd done forty-two.

T: Is that the greatest number it could possibly be?

C: No, it's not. Fifty-two – that works too!

T: Can you explain why?

C: I can have fifty-two even though the tens are the same, because the ones is less.

T: Good.

For children who need support, how could you make sure they see which digit is missing, and its relative value?

Can you convince me that twelve was a logical starting point? How could you explain it to another child who was unsure where to start?

Can you explain why you stopped looking for more possibilities when you reached forty-two?

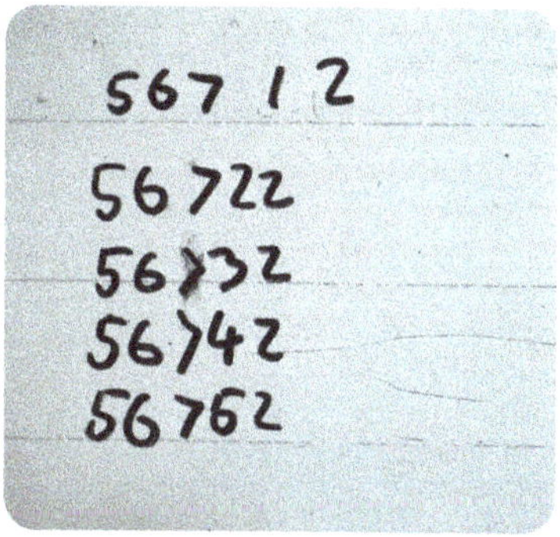

▲ This child systematically records possible statements that would make 56 > □ 2 true.

What next?

Give children a set of incorrect statements and ask them what they could change to make them correct.

Needing support

Look and listen for children who are not confident reading a statement containing the < and > symbols.

This child has written 44 < 84, 44 < 94 and 88 < 4.

(Teacher points to <.)

T: Do you know what this means?

C: No.

T: Can I draw something to help you?

(Teacher draws a diagram with the < and > symbols, labelled 'less than' and 'greater than'.)

T: This means less than, (points to < symbol) and this means greater than (points to > symbol). Which one does your symbol match?

(Teacher points to < in 44 < 84.)

C: This one.

(Child points to < in the teacher's diagram.)

T: Yes. That's 'less than'. Say the whole sentence.

C: Forty-four is less than eighty-four.

T: Do you agree with that?

C: Yes.

T: How could you check?

(Child makes 44 and 84 using base-ten apparatus.)

T: Which one's less?

(Child points to 44.)

C: This one has four tens and that has eight tens, so this is less.

T: Great explaining. Let's try another one. What does this say?

(Teacher points to 88 < 4.)

C: Eighty-eight is less than four.

T: Do you agree?

C: No, because both the ones and tens are more.

(Child corrects to 88 > 4.)

C: Eighty-eight is greater than four.

What can you tell me about these numbers?

▲ This child has written 44 < 84, 44 < 94 and 88 < 4. The teacher draws a diagram of the < > symbols with base-ten inside to help.

How do we know that forty-four is less than eighty-eight? What can we see from the digits in the numbers?

Needing support

Look and listen for children finding only one possible digit to make a statement correct.

This child is working on 44 < □4. They have recorded one example: 44 < 54.

Can you explain to me why you chose to put a five in the tens column?

T: Can you write another? What are you using to show your thinking?

C: *Base-ten.*

T: You need a number that's greater than forty-four but has four ones. What could we start with?

C: *Forty-eight?*

T: Let's think about that. Can you make it for me?

(Child makes 48 with base-ten apparatus.)

T: What can you tell me about the ones?

C: *There are eight. Oh, I've got to have four ones.*

T: Try making forty-four, and then we'll see what we can do.

(Child makes 44, then adds 4 tens.)

T: Great! What number have you made?

C: *Eighty-four.*

T: Can you write the statement?

(Child writes 44 < 84.)

T: What have you shown me with the base-ten?

C: *Forty-four is less than eighty-four.*

Can we tell from the words that forty-four is less than eighty-four?

What next?

Ask children to check their statements by building the numbers with base-ten apparatus laid end to end.

How does building the numbers using base-ten apparatus convince ourselves that one number is greater or less than another?

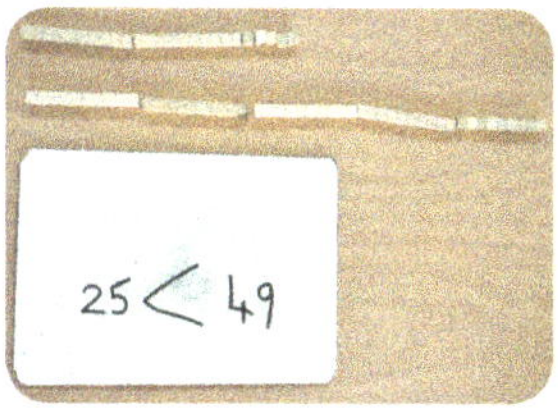

◀ The layout of the base-ten apparatus supports the child in making a visual comparison between the two numbers.

Going deeper

Give children incorrect statements and ask them to correct them by replacing one digit only. Tell them they must change the digit so the two numbers are as close to each other (e.g. on a 100-square) as they can be, e.g. given 79 < 32 they could change to 29 < 32 or 79 < 82 (difference of 3).

Children are working on 79 < 32.

T: At the moment, it says that seventy-nine is less than thirty-two. So change one of those digits for me, so that the statement is correct.

C: *I've done one.*

(Child has written 39 < 32.)

T: Let's have a look. Read that for me?

C: *Thirty-nine is greater than thirty-two.*

T: So what's this symbol here?

C: *Greater than. Oh! No, it's less than.*

T: OK, have another go.

(Child changes to 79 < 82.)

T: OK, read it to me then. What does this say?

C: *Seventy-nine is less than eighty-two.*

T: Why did you change that digit?

C: *Because the tens need to be higher, because you couldn't make the ones higher.*

T: Good, lovely clear language. And why did you choose eighty-two and not a different number of tens?

C: *Because eighty is the closest ten that is higher than seventy.*

T: Good explaining. What's the difference between the value of seventy-nine and eighty-two?

C: *The difference is three.*

T: Three, yes. So could you make the difference any less than three?

C: *Yes.*

Which apparatus or representations would be helpful here? What would a picture add to the child's reasoning?

T: Great. Have a try.

(Child records 79 < 80.)

C: So eighty is bigger than seventy-nine, and the difference is one.

T: Yes, but you can only change one digit, and if you've got eighty, you've changed two digits. Annoying, isn't it? So let's put thirty-two back there and see if you can change a different digit so that the statement makes sense.

(Child writes 29 < 32.)

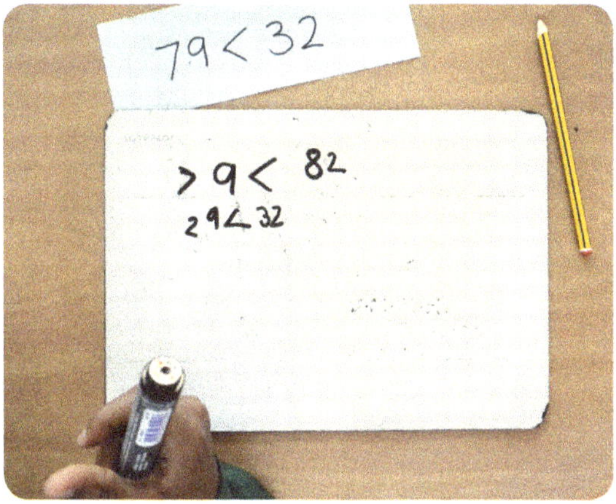

◀ This child has recorded: 79 < 82 and 29 < 32. Support children to write numbers clearly so, e.g. 7 is not confused with >.

T: Can you show me this with apparatus?

(Child builds 29 and 32.)

C: Twenty-nine is shorter than thirty-two.

T: So you've come up with two pairs of numbers. Which one of these do you think has the smallest difference?

(Teacher points to 79 < 82 and 29 < 32.)

T: Which two numbers are the closest?

C: They're both the same.

T: How do you know that?

C: Because eighty-two take away three is seventy-nine, and thirty-two take away three is twenty-nine.

> This child is making a rich connection here between value and measurement. This could be shared with the class.

What next?

Ask children to work in pairs and write similar problems for each other.

Chapter 2
Addition and subtraction

Strand overview

Aims

Children consolidate recall of number facts to 20 and begin to develop fluency with adding and subtracting 2-digit numbers. They reason about how knowledge of adding and subtracting single digits can be applied to multiples of 10. They solve problems of increasing complexity, particularly ones where the 'unknown' in a problem is not always in an obvious place.

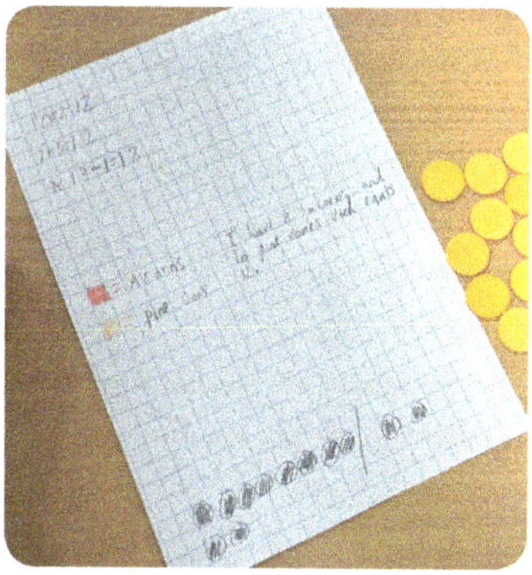

Key ideas

- Three core experiences give rise to addition and subtraction. First, change increase (There are 27 children in the hall and more arrive. Now there are 46. How many arrived?) /change decrease (There are some children in the playground, 8 go back into school. Now there are 27 children in the playground. How many were there to start with?). Second, collection (46 children are in the hall. 27 are girls. How many are boys?). Third, comparison (46 children are in the playground. There are 27 more in the hall. How many children in the hall?). Children need to learn how to identify and name each type of problem.
- Children should view all addition and subtraction situations as part-part-whole relationships. This helps them model, visualize and describe the relationship between addition and subtraction.
- Addition and subtraction problems can take the form 'start, change, result' e.g. in 15 – □ = 7, the start is 15, the (unknown) change is – 8, and the result is 7. Children find problems easiest when the result is the unknown.
- Additions can be checked by summing the addends in a different order, and subtractions with a 'related' addition.
- Understanding and using decomposition (e.g. exchanging 1 ten for 10 ones) when subtracting one 2-digit number from another is based on a sound understanding of place value.

Models and apparatus

Children will benefit from modelling problems using concrete apparatus such as 10-frames. A part-part-whole or bar model will help them identify the relationship between the numbers. Having identified the relationship, a number line supports them in carrying out the calculation.

View the video on the Year 2 Teacher Support area of the Digital Planner

Progression through the National Curriculum

Year 1

- Read, write and interpret mathematical statements involving addition (+), subtraction (–) and equals (=) signs.
- Represent and use number bonds and related subtraction facts within 20.
- Add and subtract 1-digit and 2-digit numbers to 20, including zero.
- Solve one-step problems that involve addition and subtraction, using concrete objects and pictorial representations, and missing number problems such as 7 = □ – 9.

Year 2

- Solve problems with addition and subtraction:
  - using concrete objects and pictorial representations, including those involving numbers, quantities and measures
  - applying their increasing knowledge of mental and written methods.
- Recall and use addition and subtraction facts to 20 fluently, and derive and use related facts up to 100.
- Add and subtract numbers using concrete objects, pictorial representations, and mentally, including:
  - a 2-digit number and ones
  - a 2-digit number and tens
  - two 2-digit numbers
  - adding three 1-digit numbers.
- Show that addition of two numbers can be done in any order (commutative) and subtraction of one number from another cannot.
- Recognize and use the inverse relationship between addition and subtraction and use this to check calculations and solve missing number problems.

Year 3

- Add and subtract numbers mentally, including:
  - a 3-digit number and ones
  - a 3-digit number and tens
  - a 3-digit number and hundreds.
- Add and subtract numbers with up to three digits, using formal written methods of columnar addition and subtraction.
- Estimate the answer to a calculation and use inverse operations to check answers.
- Solve problems, including missing number problems, using number facts, place value, and more complex addition and subtraction.

Year 2 sub-objectives

Term 1

- Solve problems with addition and subtraction using concrete objects and pictorial representations, including those involving numbers, quantities and measures.
- Represent and use number bonds within 20.
- Recall and use addition and subtraction facts to 20 fluently.
- Add a 2-digit number and ones using concrete objects, pictorial representations, and mentally.
- Add three 1-digit numbers using concrete objects, pictorial representations, and mentally.
- Show that addition of two numbers can be done in any order (commutative) and subtraction of one number from another cannot.
- Recognize and use the inverse relationship between addition and subtraction and use this to solve missing number problems.

Term 2

- Solve problems with addition and subtraction using concrete objects and pictorial representations, including those involving numbers, quantities and measures.
- Recall and use addition and subtraction facts to 20 fluently.
- Derive and use related facts up to 100.
- Add and subtract a 2-digit number and tens using concrete objects, pictorial representations, and mentally.
- Add and subtract two 2-digit numbers using concrete objects, pictorial representations, and mentally.
- Show that addition of two numbers can be done in any order (commutative) and subtraction of one number from another cannot.
- Recognize and use the inverse relationship between addition and subtraction and use this to solve missing number problems.

Term 3

- Solve problems with addition and subtraction by applying increasing knowledge of mental and written methods.
- Recall and use addition and subtraction facts to 20 fluently.
- Derive and use related facts up to 100.
- Add and subtract two 2-digit numbers using concrete objects, pictorial representations, and mentally.
- Recognize and use the inverse relationship between addition and subtraction and use this to check calculations.

Tasks in Practice

Launch task: Let's get ready for winter

DP Year 2 > Term 1 > Unit 2 > Addition and subtraction > Week 4 > Launch task

In this task, children pretend they are squirrels gathering acorns and pine cones, using up to 20 cubes or counters of two colours. They record this using number sentences and part-part-whole models or bar models.

On track

Children who are 'on track' make and represent additions. They use cubes or counters to show that they can change the addends (the parts) in the problem while keeping the sum (the whole) the same.

Groups of children have been given an amount (between 11 and 20) of double-sided counters to represent the squirrel's tasty treats. They need to find as many different combinations of acorns and pine cones as they can for their number of tasty treats. The teacher and children agree to use the red side of the counters to represent acorns and the yellow side for pine cones.

T: So, how many have you got altogether?

C: Twelve.

T: Can you draw a part-part-whole model to show what you've done? Where would you write twelve?

(Child writes 12.)

T: What are your two addends?

C: Six.

T: Can you add that to your part-part-whole model?

(Child writes 6 as one part.)

C: And six.

(Child writes the second 6.)

Modelling precise vocabulary helps children acquire and use it themselves.

T: So you've got six acorns and six ...

C: Pine cones. And altogether we've got twelve.

T: Good. Is there another way? You've done six and six, and earlier in the lesson I did five and seven. What is another way?

C: So, eight plus six ... no, eight plus four ... so we need colours.

T: Show me with your counters.

(Child sets out 8 red counters and 4 yellow.)

C: There are twelve counters.

T: Great. Is there another way? Show me.

▲ This child recorded a whole of twelve with parts: 6 and 6, 4 and 8, and 5 and 7, which they have also made with counters.

▲ This child has moved on to pairs to 20, recording their work systematically.

What next?

Children make and then draw all the ways of making a total of 8 and of 9, and then say what is the same and what is different. Draw out that 8 is a double (of 4), but 9 is not.

How could pictorial representations help with looking at doubles?

Needing support

Look and listen for children who are not reliably counting correctly the numbers of counters representing the addends and the sum. Listen and look for mistakes (e.g. missing out items, omitting to say a number when counting up from 1 or not counting with one-to-one correspondence).

This child struggles to count how many counters they have. The teacher works with them using a 10-frame for support.

T: We're using red counters for the acorns and yellow for the pine cones.

(Teacher shows 19 yellow counters and 1 red counter.)

T: How many pine cones have you got? Can you count them?

C: *One, two, three ...*

(Child counts the counters out onto the table.)

C: *Nineteen.*

T: One is an acorn. How many pine cones?

C: *Twenty.*

T: There's twenty altogether. One is an acorn. How many pine cones?

C: *Two.*

T: You think you've only got two yellow counters? Let's see, shall we make a group of ten?

C: *Yes.*

(Child puts out eleven yellow counters.)

C: *That's ten.*

T: How do you know that's ten? Shall we count them?

C: *One, two [...] ten, eleven.*

T: So close, good estimating. Shall we take one away?

(Child removes 1 counter to leave 10. Child writes 10.)

T: How many are left over here?

C: *One, two [...] eight, nine.*

If the child has counting difficulties, a bead string might support them to see the stable sum of 20. Show 20 beads and ask children to slide one bead along the string for each acorn, leaving the pine cones together. *How many tasty treats altogether?*

T: You've got nine? Shall we put them in a 10-frame to check? What do we have to remember about 10-frames?

C: *One counter in each box.*

(Child puts the 9 counters in a 10-frame.)

T: How many yellow pine cones have you got here?

C: *Nine.*

(Child writes 9 with support.)

T: So how many yellow pine cones have you got altogether? You have one group of ten, plus another nine. How many is that?

C: *Nineteen.*

T: And how many red acorns do I have?

C: *One.*

T: Can you say the number sentence: nineteen plus ... ?

C: *Nineteen plus one equals twenty.*

T: Good. Now I'm going to change one yellow pine cone into a red acorn, so there are two red acorns. How many yellow pine cones are there now?

C: *Eighteen.*

▲ The child records 9 yellow pine cones with support.

What might you do if a child counted on in ones from 9?

Have I added or removed any counters? Do we still have the same total?

What next?

Ask children to show three different ways of making the total of 8, using a 10-frame (or bead string) to support their counting and reasoning.

Going deeper

Ask children to describe any patterns they notice in their addends, and to explore this for different totals. Listen for their reasoning why the patterns are as they observe them.

The teacher and the child discuss the patterns the child found when recording possible combinations for 20 tasty treats. The child started with 20 pine cones and zero acorns and changed one pine cone for an acorn each time.

C: *I noticed that on the acorns it goes one, two, three. It goes up. And with the pine cones the numbers go down.*

T: Do they go up in ones? Twos?

C: *They go in ones.*

T: So what happened on the acorn side?

C: *We added one.*

T: Good. So if we added one more acorn, what would happen to the pine cones?

(Teacher points to addends 2 and 18.)

C: *It would become seventeen.*

T: Why seventeen? What did you do?

C: *Because I counted back one from eighteen.*

T: OK, so you counted backwards, in ones. And you counted up in ones. But your whole was always twenty. Can you say in a sentence what you've noticed?

C: *This goes up in ones, this goes down in ones.*

T: Tell me that again, but talking about acorns and pine cones.

C: *I have one more acorn and one less pine cone.*

T: What about the total, twenty?

C: *I have one more acorn and one less pine cone but the sum is always twenty.*

T: Did you notice the same sort of pattern with twenty-three?

C2: *Yes.*

T: Do you want to come and demonstrate it?

(Child 2 records on the board pairs to 23.)

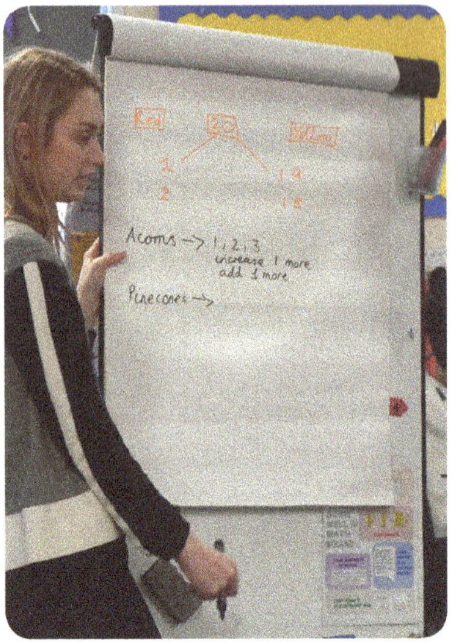

▲ The teacher has drawn a part-part-whole model and is changing addends underneath.

▲ This child systematically records number sentences for pairs to 23.

T: Oh, twenty-three add zero! What does that mean?

C2: One squirrel got no acorns.

T: OK! Can we start to see the same patterns as we found for 20 here with 23? Look at the numbers.

C2: We're subtracting these in ones.

T: And this side?

C2: They're going up in ones.

T: And the total?

C2: It's not changing, it's always twenty-three.

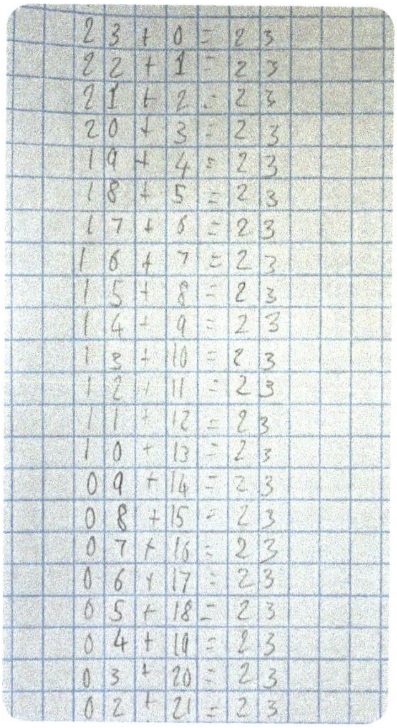

▲ A child's recording of pairs to 23.

▲ Pairs to 20. Working systematically, this child records numbers 1–20 in the left-hand column before recording numbers 19–0 in the right-hand column.

What next?

How many different ways are there to make 12, with two addends? Don't forget about 0! What about if we use three addends? Do you think there will be more or fewer? What about if we use four addends?

Can you select a number between 10 and 20 and find out how many ways there are to make it with:

2 addends

3 addends and

4 addends?

'Predict and then verify' is a rich prompt for developing deeper thinking.

Tasks in Practice

Learning task 3: Find the missing number

DP Year 2 > Term 2 > Unit 8 > Addition and subtraction > Week 2 > Learning task 3

In this task, children use known facts to solve missing number problems.

On track

Children who are 'on track' identify the parts and wholes in a missing number sentence and use this, along with their knowledge of number facts to 10, to calculate unknowns.

Children are working on 30 + ? = 80.

C: *So we're going to get eighty.* (Child shows 80 on a bead string.) *And we're going to take away thirty. One, two, three!* (Child moves three blocks of 10 along the bead string.)

T: Three what?

C: *Tens, three tens. And so that's fifty. One, two, three, four, five tens.* (Child counts 5 blocks of 10 on the bead string.) *And then, how many more do we need? So we need thirty. One, two, three, four, five, six, seven, eight, yes!* (Child counts the 8 blocks of 10 on the bead string.) *To make a hundred you need two more.*

T: So we've got the eighty, and then what do we do?

C: *We subtract thirty. One, two, three. One two, three, four, five. So we think it might be fifty.*

T: And can you explain what you've done there?

(Teacher points to child's board, on which she has drawn 8 lines, crossed out 3, and circled the remaining 5.)

C: *So eighty is the biggest number, so we drew eight. And then crossed out three.*

How is the use of the inverse (doing and undoing the calculation with the beads) supporting the child's ability to solve missing number problems?

Would a different representation (10-frames or base-ten apparatus) work as well here?

T: Three what?

C: *Three tens! These represent tens* (child points to the lines), *and then we know it's equal to fifty, so eighty subtract thirty is equal to fifty.*

T: And what are the wholes and what are the parts in that calculation?

C: *The wholes ... There's only one whole!*

T: Well done! So what is the whole?

C: *The whole is eighty, and the two parts are thirty and fifty.*

The teacher draws out precise language from the child.

Consider how the opportunities for working with parts and wholes over time have contributed to the child's success here.

What next?

Children work on further missing number problems in pairs that use multiples of 10. They model their approach and share their reasoning with the class.

Notice the variation in the tasks: first 30 + ? = 80, then ? + 30 = 90. What are the advantages and potential disadvantages of this?

◀ This child has solved several missing number addition and subtraction problems, and shown her reasoning using bar models.

Needing support

Look and listen for children who do not correctly identify the parts and wholes in a missing number sentence.

Children are working on 100 – ? = 40.

T: So you have the numbers forty and one hundred. What do you think the missing number could be?

C: *Sixty!*

T: Sixty? Why do you think that?

C: *Because it equals to sixty!*

T: Can you write a number sentence? Forty, sixty and one hundred. Are you going to write it as an addition or a subtraction?

C: *Subtraction. No, no, addition.*

T: Write your number sentence and explain to me why you think it's addition and not subtraction?

(Child writes 40 + 60 = 100.)

T: Forty plus sixty. Can you show that on your bead string?

(Child starts counting beads in ones.)

T: Do you need to count each bead individually? Is that the quickest way?

C: *Ten. Oh, I could count in tens?*

(Child counts 4 tens and separates off 40 beads.)

T: So how many beads are on the other side?

(Child counts 6 tens)

C: *Sixty.*

T: Forty plus sixty – are those our parts or our wholes?

C: *Wholes.*

T: Forty plus sixty are our wholes? Are you sure? Can you draw that for me in a part-part-whole model?

(Teacher draws a part-part-whole model for the child to fill in. Child fills in 100, 40 and 60.)

Does this child see the equals sign as 'where the answer goes'? In this case, they may be saying 'it equals to sixty' because that's the answer for the missing box.

The teacher doesn't say that any answer is wrong, but also doesn't say if it's correct. What might be the reasons for doing so?

T: What are our parts?

C: *Forty and sixty.*

▲ The child correctly completes the part-part-whole model. How is this notation supporting the child with the language here?

T: What other equations could we write using these numbers?

C: *If I know forty plus sixty then four plus six.*

(Child holds up a bead string showing 11 beads.)

T: Ooh, is this four plus six? Shall we count together?

(Child counts beads, and adjusts to show 4 and 6.)

T: What is four plus six equal to?

C: *Ten!*

T: Good. So if I know four plus six is equal to ten, then what else do we know?

C: *Forty plus sixty is a hundred!*

How much time should we spend linking facts to demonstrate relationships?

What next?

Children solve further missing number problems with multiples of ten. Support identifying the parts and wholes using the part-part-whole model. Consider placing base-10 apparatus on the diagram.

Going deeper

Give children more challenging addition and subtraction calculations, e.g. vary the position of the unknown or include two unknowns. E.g. 40 = 100 – ?, ? – ? = 30, ? – 30 = ?

Children are working on ? – ? = 30.

T: Can you explain that to me?

C: *Well I thought it was ninety subtract sixty equals thirty, because I know that nine subtract six equals three.*

T: Great fact use. What is your whole and what are your parts?

C: *Well, the whole is ninety and the parts are sixty and thirty.*

T: Can you do another calculation that gets you to thirty? What other tens numbers could the question marks be?

C: *Forty subtract ten!*

T: That's a really nice one. Can you write that down?

(Child writes 40 – 10, then 50 – 20 and 60 – 30.)

The child is concentrating on multiples of 10. This brings the deeper structure to the surface, which might be less obvious with 'random' examples, such as 41 – 11 = 30, 53 – 23 = 30.

T: What are you doing there?

C: *I'm adding ten. If I know forty subtract ten equals thirty, then I know fifty subtract twenty equals thirty and sixty subtract thirty equals thirty. I'm adding ten every time.*

T: What are you adding ten to?

Consider using a number line to demonstrate why the difference of 30 is maintained by increasing the other numbers (the minuend and subtrahend) by 10 each time.

C: The whole and the part that isn't thirty.

T: Do you think you've found them all?

C: Yes!

T: Could you have a calculation where one of these question marks was thirty?

C: Oh! Thirty subtract zero equals thirty!

T: Good thinking. I like that you corrected yourself. How many do you think there are? How many possible numbers are there for those question marks?

C: Umm ... I'd say about ten.

T: That's an interesting answer, why do you think there's ten? Do you want to have a go and see if you're right?

(Child starts to record some more calculations.)

C: Oh, no, wait, there could be way more than ten!

T: Why is that?

C: Because if you went up to like a thousand there are so many numbers you could subtract to get thirty!

Children often forget the zero examples.

Notice that this child deduces further examples from the selection they have found.

What next?

What is the maximum number of possibilities for ? – ? = 30 if you can only use multiples of 10 and neither of the numbers can be more than 100?

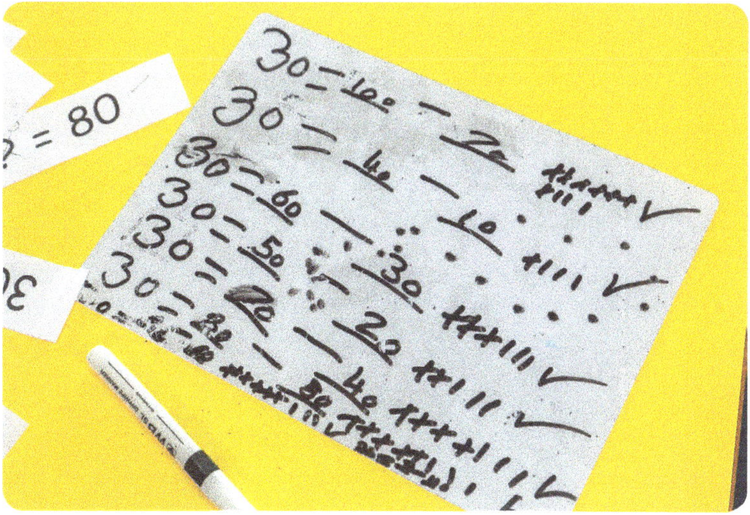

This child has reasoned pictorially as well as numerically, showing confidence expressing themselves mathematically in more than one way.

◀ This child has found six out of seven possibilities. How could they be prompted to work systematically?

Tasks in Practice

Learning task 2: Planting seeds

DP Year 2 > Term 3 > Unit 16 > Addition and subtraction > Week 3 > Learning task 2

In this task, children use decomposition when subtracting a 1-digit or 2-digit number from another 2-digit number.

On track

Children who are 'on track' subtract two 2-digit numbers by partitioning the subtrahend and subtracting first the tens and then the ones, e.g. 45 – 32 = 45 – 30 – 2. (In this calculation, '32' is the subtrahend.)

Example 1

Children start by subtracting a 1-digit number from a 2-digit number: 33 – 8.

T: What's the whole?

C: *Thirty-three.*

T: How do we show the problem on a number line?

C: *Start at thirty-three and take away eight.*

T: Is there a better way?

C: *Take away three first.*

T: Why take away three first?

C: *Because taking away eight ones would take ages. It's quicker to make bigger jumps.*

T: If we take away three, what number do we get to?

C: *Thirty.*

(Child draws jump back from 33 to 30 and labels it – 3.)

T: What now?

C: *What you add to three to make eight is what you need to take away now from thirty. That's five.*

T: Good reasoning! Show me?

(Child draws jump back from 30 to 25 and labels it – 5.)

C: *Take away five from thirty to get twenty-five.*

T: Can you record the calculation?

(Child writes 33 – 8 = 25.)

If the child did not see 8 as 3 and 5, how could you support them in finding a sensible way to partition 8 for this calculation?

Why does jumping back to a multiple of 10 on the number line help us to work out the calculation?

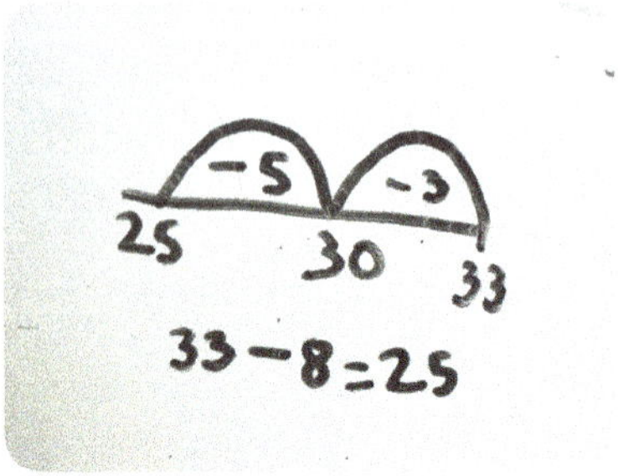

Example 2

Children move onto subtracting a 2-digit number from a 2-digit number. They are working on 42 – 16. They make 42 using 10-frames and counters.

T: How are you going to take away sixteen?

C: *By taking away a ten.*

T: Lovely, take away the whole ten.

(Child takes away a whole 10-frame.)

C: *Then you take away the two.*

(Child takes away frame with 2 counters.)

C: *Then you take away four from this one.*

(Child takes away 4 from a full 10-frame.)

Is it easier if you subtract the ten first, or the six first? Can you explain why?

◀ This child has taken away one full 10-frame, and then the frame containing 2 counters. He now takes 4 counters from one of the remaining frames.

T: Why did you take away four?

C: *Because two add four equals six and then there's ten.*

T: And that makes ...?

C: *Six add ten is sixteen.*

T: Lovely explaining. I really like how you've shown me what to do with the 10-frames. So what's left?

C: *Twenty-six.*

Secure knowledge of bonds within 10 is crucial for developing fluency here.

What next?

Ask children to write a subtraction sentence taking a 2-digit number from another 2-digit number and give it to their partner to solve.

Needing support

Look and listen for children who count back in ones rather than partitioning the ones of the subtrahend (the number being subtracted) to enable them to bridge to the preceding ten.

This child is working on 26 – 8. They remove 8 counters from a full 10-frame instead of partitioning.

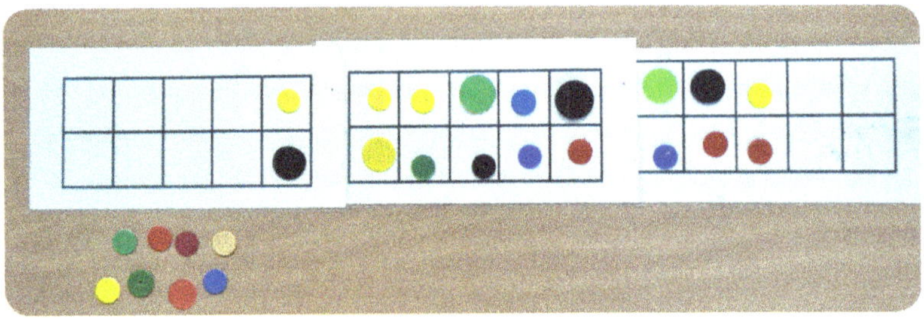

Why did you remove the counters from that frame?

T: You've done twenty-six take away eight. How many are left?

(Child starts to count the remaining counters.)

T: Can I stop you there? Your counting is lovely but it takes a long time to count in ones! You've used a really nice strategy by taking the eight away from one of the tens. If I move these two counters over here (pointing to the 10-frame on the far right) we have ten and eight more. Let's put the eight counters back and try to take them away a different way.

(Child puts back the 8 counters.)

T: Thanks. Have we got any full-up frames?

C: This one and this one.

T: Yes. What do we know and like about full-up frames?

C: It's ten.

T: Yes, and we don't have to count. We want to take away eight. What would be the easiest way of doing that? Instead of taking away eight ones, can we take away any of the frames?

C: That one.

(Child points to the frame with 6 counters.)

T: Good, we could take this whole frame away, couldn't we? How many is that?

If you think children are not secure with the concept that 8 can be partitioned into 6 and 2, what quick task could you do at this point to remind them of the number facts for 8?

C: *Six.*

(Child removes the 6 counters.)

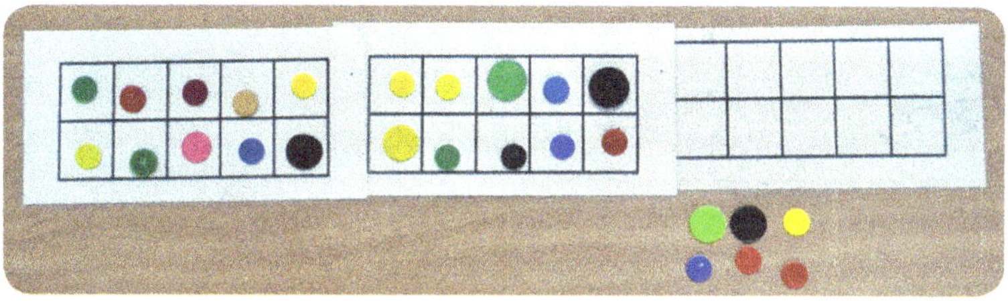

T: How many more do we need to take away to take away our eight?

C: *Two.*

T: Great. Which two do you want to take away?

C: *These two.*

(Child takes away 2 counters.)

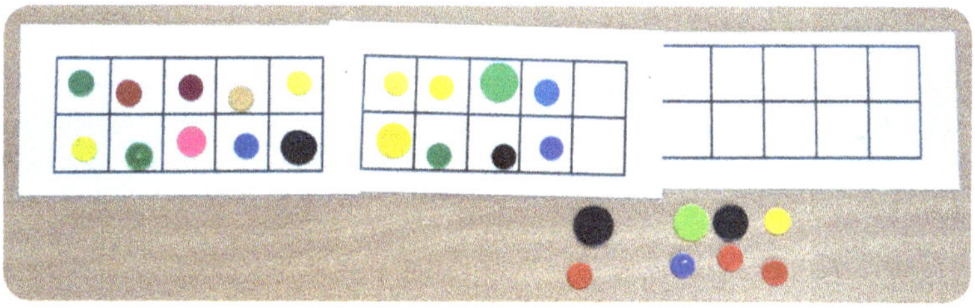

T: I was thinking exactly the same. What's left?

C: *Ten and eight.*

T: How do you know that's ten?

(Teacher points to the full 10-frame.)

C: *It's full up.*

T: How do you know that's eight?

(Teacher points to the 10-frame with 8 counters on.)

C: *Because it was ten and I took away two.*

T: Good reasoning. How many altogether?

C: *Eighteen.*

This shows that the child doesn't have to count in ones, but they still default to doing so.

What next?

Once children are confident with 10-frames and counters, ask them to use base-ten apparatus, then number lines.

Why is confidence with 10-frames necessary before working with base-ten apparatus?

Going deeper

Max is calculating 64 – 9 = □. He says: Nine is six and three, so I'll take away six then take away three. What advice would you give him?

T: Do you agree with the way Max is working, or not? And why?

C: No, it's not the easiest way to do it. We could do sixty-four minus ten then add one.

T: Can you explain why? Sixty-four take away ten would be ...

C: Fifty-four. Then add one so it's fifty-five.

T: Great method. What else would be another good way of doing that?

C: So you have sixty-four and then you take away the four and then you have sixty, and then on the nine you take away the five left over and then you've got your answer, fifty-five.

T: Good thinking. So why wouldn't you take away a three and a six? That's still nine.

C: Because if you take away a three from sixty-four it will make it sixty-one, and then take away six from sixty-one ... it's a bit trickier than taking away five from sixty.

T: Great reasoning. Can you show me on your number lines why your suggestions are easier than Max's?

How did you know you could take away 10 and then add 1? Can you think of a really clear way to show this method to another child?

Are children confident with partitioning all numbers to 10? If not, what could you do to improve their conceptual understanding and rapid recall?

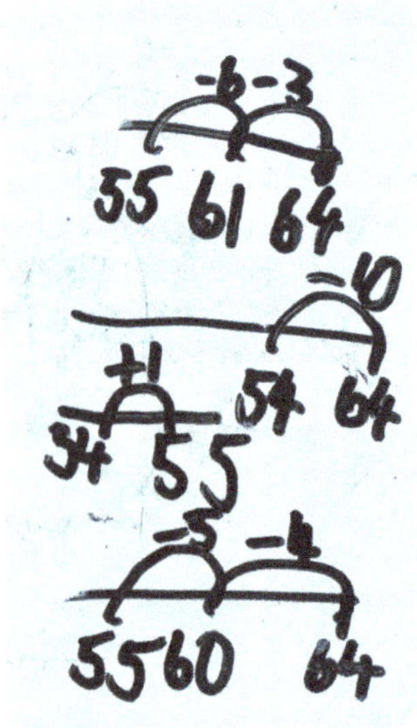

◀ This child uses number lines to compare three methods for 64 – 9:
64 – 3 = 61 and 61 – 6 = 55
64 – 10 = 54 and 54 + 1 = 55
64 – 4 = 60 and 60 – 5 = 55

C: *This first one is where I tried Max's way. It looks quite easy on the number line because it's only two jumps, but it's harder because it doesn't stop at sixty.*

T: What does this number line show?

C: *Sixty-four take away ten equals fifty-four, and then I just plussed one on this number line here.*

T: So you've used two number lines to make it clearer on your board. Thank you, that's really helpful.

C: *And that last one is where I took away four and then five. It's easier than Max's because it jumps back to a multiple of ten first. It's easy to take away from a multiple of ten.*

Which of the methods you tried do you feel is the best approach for this calculation? Can you explain your reasoning?

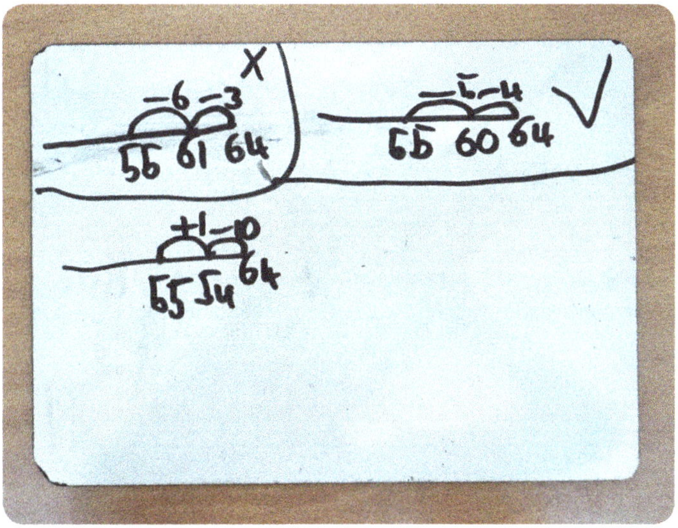

▲ What would you say to a child who had represented 64 – 10 + 1 on the number line in this way?

What next?

Ask children to think of a subtraction involving two 2-digit numbers. Their partner shows different ways of calculating the answer then explains which method they think is easiest and why.

Chapter 3
Multiplication and division

Strand overview

Aims

Children count fluently in multiples of 2, 3, 5 and 10. They solve multiplication problems involving simple rates and scaling, and division problems as grouping and sharing. They reason about the relationship between multiplication and division, and why multiplication is always commutative but division is not (except e.g. $2 \div 2$ or $5 \div 5$).

Key ideas

- Children are helped in their understanding of multiplication by enumerating a collection of objects by making equal groups and then skip counting.
- The convention that children work with is that, e.g. 4×5 is '4 multiplied by 5', or 5 groups of 4.
- Multiplication is much more than repeated addition. As well as simple rate problems (e.g. I read 3 pages in 1 minute. How many pages do I read in 5 minutes?), children need to see multiplication as scaling (e.g. a baby eel is 3 cm long and its mother is 5 times as long. How long is the mother?)
- Division as grouping (e.g. I have 14 sweets; I give 2 to each friend; how many friends can have sweets?) and as sharing (e.g. I share 14 sweets between 7 friends. How many sweets do they get each?) are practically and conceptually different. Grouping needs to be reinforced alongside the more familiar concept of sharing.
- Children sometimes over-generalize from realizing that multiplying in either order does not change the product to thinking that division is also commutative.

Models and apparatus

Arrays embody the commutative properties of multiplication, and represent the key idea of equal groups. Children need lots of practice making arrays and describing the relationships they see. Division problems need to be acted out so that children get a strong, embodied sense of the difference between grouping (e.g. three for you, three for you ... until the amount runs out) and sharing (e.g. one for you, one for you ... until everyone has an equal amount).

View the video on the Year 2 Teacher Support area of the Digital Planner

Progression through the National Curriculum

Year 1

- Solve one-step problems involving multiplication and division, by calculating the answer using concrete objects, pictorial representations and arrays with the support of the teacher.

Year 2

- Recall and use multiplication and division facts for the 2, 5 and 10 multiplication tables, including recognizing odd and even numbers.
- Calculate mathematical statements for multiplication and division within the multiplication tables and write them using the multiplication (×), division (÷) and equals (=) signs.
- Show that multiplication of two numbers can be done in any order (commutative) and division of one number by another cannot.
- Solve problems involving multiplication and division, using materials, arrays, repeated addition, mental methods, and multiplication and division facts, including problems in contexts.

Year 3

- Recall and use multiplication and division facts for the 3, 4 and 8 multiplication tables.
- Write and calculate mathematical statements for multiplication and division using the multiplication tables that they know, including for 2-digit numbers times 1-digit numbers, using mental and progressing to formal written methods.
- Solve problems, including missing number problems, involving multiplication and division, including positive integer scaling problems and correspondence problems in which n objects are connected to m objects.

Year 2 sub-objectives

Term 1

- Recall and use multiplication and division facts for the 2 multiplication table, and begin practising counting in threes.
- Recall and use multiplication and division facts for the 5 and 10 multiplication tables.
- Recognize odd and even numbers.
- Solve problems involving multiplication and division, using materials and arrays, including problems in contexts.

Term 2

- Calculate mathematical statements for multiplication and division within the multiplication tables and write them using the multiplication (×), division (÷) and equals (=) signs.
- Show that multiplication of two numbers can be done in any order (commutative) and division of one number by another cannot.
- Solve problems involving multiplication and division, using materials and arrays, including problems in contexts.

Term 3

- Solve problems involving multiplication and division, using materials, arrays, repeated addition, mental methods, and multiplication and division facts, including problems in contexts.

Tasks in Practice

Learning task 1: Sharing problems

DP Year 2 > Term 1 > Unit 3 > Multiplication and division > Week 6 > Learning task 1

In this task, children represent sharing contexts when a dividend and a divisor have a whole number quotient, and when they don't. They explore, when sharing, whether there is a remainder or not.

On track

Children who are 'on track' show when a quantity can and can't be shared into equal groups.

Children are considering this problem:

- 7 friends are buying stickers to share equally between themselves. They could buy a pack of 25 stickers, a pack of 22 stickers or a pack of 21 stickers. What pack should the friends buy, so that they can share the stickers equally?

C: *We think they should buy twenty-one stickers.*

T: How do you know that twenty-one divides into equal groups when shared between seven friends?

C: *Three, six, nine, twelve, fifteen, eighteen, twenty-one.*

(Children count the seven groups of three cubes they have made.)

The cubes show that the groups are equal even if children are not yet confident skip counting in threes.

◀ Can you show me on your model how you know that all of the 7 friends got the same number of stickers?

T: Good, so we know that the pack of twenty-one stickers can be shared equally between seven children, and we can see this in our array. Did you make an array for 22 stickers? What did you notice?

(Children make an array with 7 rows of 3 and an eighth row with 1 cube in.)

T: Is this an equal array?

C: No.

T: That's right. What is unequal about it?

C: There are twenty-two and we want it to be equal, so we would need to take away one to make it equal.

T: Which one shall we take away?

(Child points to the single cube.)

T: Can you put it somewhere else and make all groups equal?

(Children try.)

C: No.

T: Yes, so this one extra cube means the groups aren't equal. We cannot give this one to any of the friends and still have equal groups. We call this one a remainder of one. Why do we call this a remainder of one?

C: Because it's on its own.

T: Yes, as only one remains. Can you record four number sentences for sharing twenty-one stickers?

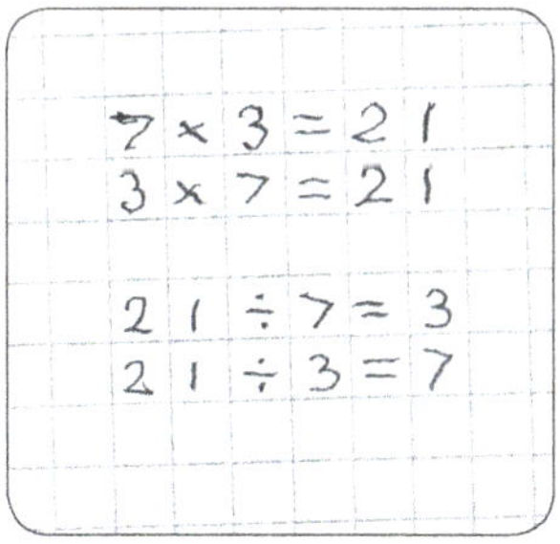

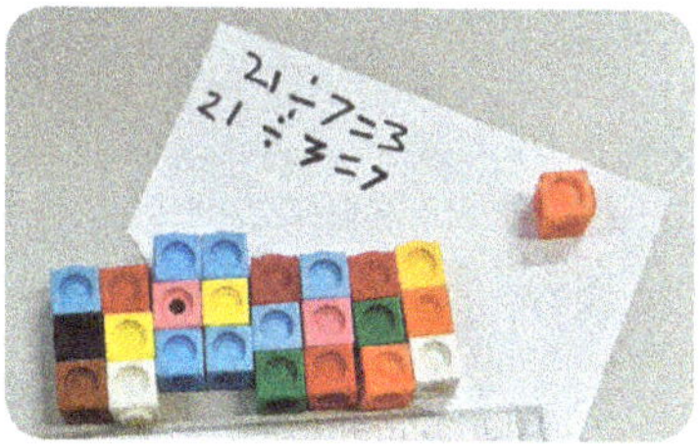

Where on your model is the bit that shows that 22 stickers cannot be shared equally between 7 friends?

Is it fair to share 22 stickers between 7 children? Why?

Number sentence frames might be useful here:

__ × __ = __

__ ÷ __ = __

What next?

What if there were 5 friends – would they choose the same pack of 21 stickers to share equally? Why? What about for a pack of 25 stickers? Why? Children build arrays and write the related calculations each time to find the solution.

Needing support

Look and listen for children who do not interpret 'equal groups' as meaning 'the same number in each group', attempting instead to share the remainder and so create unequal groups, or to count the remainder as another group. Also look and listen for children who focus on the groups' size rather than the number of groups when sharing.

T: So you think twenty-five stickers could be shared equally between seven friends? Let's see. What do you need to do?

C: Let's give them six stickers each.

(Children share out 25 cubes into groups of 6. They make 4 groups of 6 and 1 left over.)

T: How many friends are there?

C: Four.

T: How many friends are there supposed to be?

C: Seven!

T: So that means four friends have a lot of stickers, one friend has one sticker and two friends have nothing! What else could we try?

C: Let's try eight stickers each.

(Children try creating groups of 8 cubes, and find that they can only make 3 groups, with 1 left over.)

T: If six was too many in each group to share equally and it meant two people had nothing, should you be making the number in each group bigger or smaller?

C: Smaller.

T: Super. So what number of stickers shall we try giving to each friend?

How could you support children to begin with the number of groups when sharing?

You might want to model this with cubes.
Ask: *Is there a way we can share the cubes out?*

What questioning could you use here to draw out the child's reasoning that the answer will be smaller?

C: Let's try three.

T: Count in threes for me.

C: Three, six, nine [...] twenty-one, twenty-four.

(Children count out cubes in threes.)

T: So can twenty-five stickers be shared equally between seven friends, or are there any left over?

C: There's one left over.

T: How many groups of three cubes do you have?

C: One, two three, four, five, six, seven, eight, oh! So there's four left over, we need seven groups.

T: Look at the different packs of stickers on the board. What do you notice? Do twenty-one stickers work? Count in threes again and listen to the numbers that you say.

C: Three, six, nine [...] twenty-one.

(Children count out cubes in threes, making a 3 by 7 array.)

T: Can we share a pack of twenty-one stickers equally?

C: Yes!

T: How do you know?

C: There are three cubes in each group.

T: And how many friends?

C: One, two, three, four, five, six, seven. They all have three. Yes!

T: If I give you one more cube you will have twenty-two. Do you think you can share twenty-two equally between seven?

(Child places the extra cube on top of the final row of 3.)

C: No, now they don't all have the same. There is one spare.

T: We say that there's a remainder of one. Say that to me.

C: There's a remainder of one.

Confident skip counting is very important for developing understanding of multiplication.

What can we do to highlight the remainder after dividing in future examples?

What next?

Children try again with the pack of 25 stickers, sharing 25 cubes between 7 groups, to show a remainder of 4. Ask again, which pack could 7 friends share equally? Encourage children to start with a concrete or pictorial representation of the number of groups and work systematically.

Going deeper

Ask children, what number of stickers could either 5 friends or 7 friends buy so they can share stickers equally in each group. Ask for more than one example; they must convince you each time.

T: Is there a number of stickers that the five friends and also the seven friends could buy to share equally? Make sure you can convince me of your answer.

C1: Let's try sharing fourteen into five groups.

T: Why fourteen?

C1: Fourteen is double seven. So we will have seven groups of two. That means the seven friends will have 2 stickers each.

T: OK. Before you do anything, do you think you'll be able to share fourteen into five equal groups?

C2: I think no!

T: Off you go and test it.

C1: One, two, three, four, five.

(Child counts out 5 of the 14 counters, laying them out in 5 groups.)

T: OK, now share out another five.

C1: One, two, three, four, five.

(Child counts out another 5 counters, adding 1 to each of the 5 groups.)

T: Now share out another five.

C1: I can't, I've only got four.

T: So you can make five groups of two, with four remaining.

C2: They're unequal groups. So, the five friends don't have the same number of stickers. This one has less.

T: I see! What's the last digit in fourteen?

C1: Four.

T: And what did we say about multiples of five?

C2: That they all finish in five and zero.

Here the teacher has let children predict and verify. What is the impact of this?

Why is the teacher supporting children to connect this problem with prior learning?

T: OK, does fourteen finish in a five or a zero?

C1: No.

T: So is there a number of stickers that the five friends and also the seven friends could buy to share equally?

C1: It needs to end in five or zero.

T: Can you count in fives? Let's hear what numbers you say.

(Children start counting in fives.)

C2: Thirty-five! Because we shared thirty-five evenly into seven groups earlier and it also ends in five.

C2: Let's check.

(Children make a 5 by 7 array with counters.)

C1: There are five groups of seven, or seven groups of five.

T: Great. And how could we talk about stickers and friends then?

C2: Five friends have seven stickers each. And seven friends have five stickers each.

T: Good. Record that in your books with the number sentences.

▲ Children make an array for 35 with 7 groups of 5 counters.

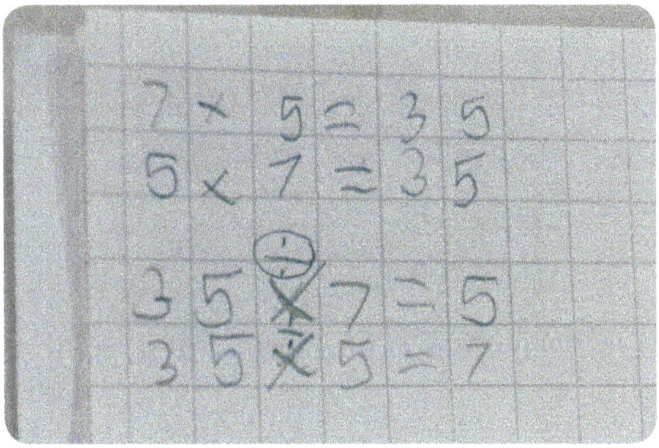

Can you think of a sharing story and a grouping story for this division number sentence?

What next?

Children find another number of stickers that the group of five friends and the group of seven friends would each be able to share equally.

Tasks in Practice

Learning task 1: Commutativity

DP Year 2 > Term 2 > Unit 11 > Multiplication and division > Week 6 > Learning task 1

In this task, children multiply two numbers in any order and show that their product stays the same.

On track

Children who are 'on track' show that multiplication is commutative, e.g. by rearranging array models where the product remains equal and the factors are the same. E.g. they say: 4 groups of 5 is 20. The factors are 4 and 5 and the product is 20. 5 groups of 4 is also 20. The factors are 5 and 4. Children say that the factors represent something different in each array.

The teacher has asked children to convince her that $8 \times 2 = 2 \times 8$.

T: Tell me about your arrays.

C1: This one is two groups of eight, and this one is eight groups of two.

◀ Children use 8 groups of 2 cubes and 2 groups of 8 cubes to show that $8 \times 2 = 2 \times 8$.

Could you and some classmates act this out, using eight mats with two children on each? How would you then rearrange yourselves to represent the other array?

T: Are they the same?

C1: Not exactly ... They both have sixteen cubes, but a different way round.

(Teacher rotates the two groups of eight 90 degrees.)

T: They look the same now, don't they?

(Teacher rotates the array back again, before turning to a different child.)

T: What number sentences have you written?

C2: Two times eight equals sixteen.

T: How else might we write this?

C3: Eight times two?

T: As a full multiplication sentence?

C2: Eight times two equals sixteen.

T: What stays the same, and what changes?

C2: The answer is always sixteen.

C3: The factors are always two and eight.

C2: Yes, but they're in different places.

T: Yes. The product, the answer, stays the same, but the order of the factors changes. So we've learned that eight times two means two groups of eight, and the product is sixteen. What have we learned about two times eight?

C4: That means eight groups of two, and that's sixteen too.

T: Brilliant. This number sentence says 'eight multiplied by two equals two multiplied by eight'. Can we say that another way?

C5: Two groups of eight is the same as eight groups of two?

T: Good, I like how you said 'is the same as'.

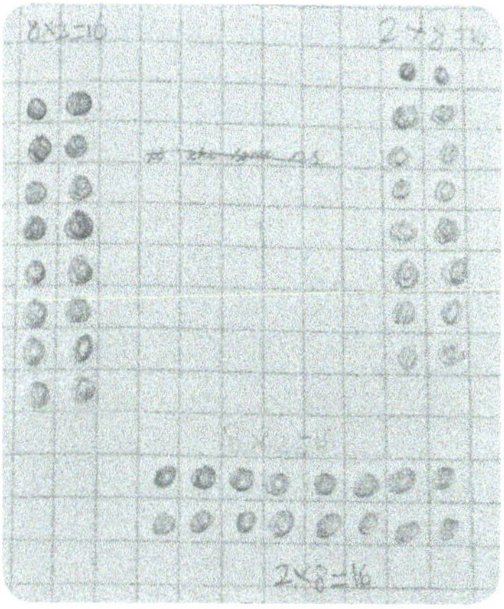

▲ This child has drawn arrays for $8 \times 2 = 2 \times 8$.

What is the same and what is different about the arrays and calculations?

Is eight times two exactly the same as two times eight?

What next?

How many more ways can you make the following true? Show me using arrays.

$2 \times \square = \square \times 2$

Needing support

Look and listen for children who do not describe the equal product in commutative array models; they focus on the differences rather than the similarities. When transforming arrays, they find the product by counting each time rather than saying they used the same number of counters to make the new array and so the product will be equal.

Children are looking at 4 × 5. The teacher gives them a frame of 5 rows.

T: This multiplication sentence means five groups of four. How would you arrange five groups of four in an array within this frame? How many rows are in the frame?

C: *One, two, three, four, five.*

T: Good. If we want five groups of four, how many cubes should go in each row?

C: *Four.*

T: OK.

(Child arranges cubes haphazardly in 4 rows.)

T: How should an array look?

C: *Equal.*

T: Equal?

C: *Equal cubes in each row.*

T: What have you got here?

C: *Five.*

T: Have you got five groups? One, two, three, four ...

(Child adds another group of 4.)

T: Now you've got five groups of four, can you make an array like on the board?

(Child connects the cubes to make 5 trains of 4.)

T: Lovely, five groups of four. If you made an array of four groups of five, how would that look?

C: *Is it just sideways?*

T: What do you mean by sideways?

C: *The same number of cubes, but turned?*

How does the supplied frame support the child in building arrays? In what other ways could this support be provided?

▲ This child uses cubes and the frame to make 5 groups of 4, before connecting the cubes into 5 sticks of 4 to make an array.

T: Shall we check? Can you use the same cubes to make four groups of five?

(Child makes 4 rows of 5 cubes.)

◀ This child uses cubes and the frame to make 4 groups of 5, before connecting the cubes into 4 sticks of 5 to make an array.

C: They're the same.

T: Yes, because you used the same cubes. So five groups of four is the same as four groups of five. Can you draw the arrays?

Can you tell me more about what is the same and what is different?

What next?

Children use number rods to compare 4 × 5 and 5 × 4. They line up five 4-rods (purple). Write 4 below each rod, then write 4 × 5 = 20. Children repeat for four 5-rods (yellow). Write 5 below each rod, then write 5 × 4 = 20. Children place the lines of rods one above the other. What do you notice about where the rods start and end up each time? Show that 4 × 5 = 5 × 4 using a tape measure.

Going deeper

Set children the word problem: *I am thinking of a number that I say when I skip count in fives and also in threes. What could the number be?* Ask children to build the related arrays. *What do you notice?*

T: Tell me what you're doing.

C: *I'm making towers of five.*

T: Why did you decide to make fives?

C: *Because I need a number that works in the three and the five times tables.*

(Child completes 3 towers of 5 and moves on to making 5 towers of 3.)

C: *Five, ten, fifteen. Fifteen cubes here, and if it equals the same on here, I'll have been right.*

(Child counts in threes to 15.)

C: *Yes, I was correct.*

T: How does that tell you that you were correct?

C: *Well, because I thought it was fifteen for the towers of three and the towers of five, and I've counted them and there's fifteen for both. I knew that they equalled the same number, but I had to check.*

T: That's great explaining. Can you move them so you can see they are the same without counting?

C: *I could put them on top of each other.*

(Child rotates the 3 towers of 5, and aligns them above the 5 towers of 3.)

The teacher doesn't assume that it's obvious what the child is doing. The child's rationale might not be what the teacher thinks it is.

Why has the teacher asked for further proof, without counting, that the product of each array is the same?

T: Good demonstration! Is there another way you could solve the problem?

C: *Probably.*

T: What other numbers do you know in the five times tables?

C: *Five, ten.*

T: OK, so if I skip counted in threes, would I get to five or ten?

C: *Three, six, nine, twelve. No.*

T: If I skip counted in threes, when would I get to the next multiple of five?

C: *... eighteen ... twenty ... No.*

T: I'm not sure what you're thinking. Can you show me?

(Child makes 4 towers of 5 cubes and 6 towers of 3 cubes.)

C: *I did another three and another five.*

T: So how many do you have?

C: *Five, ten, fifteen, twenty. Three, six, nine, twelve, fifteen, eighteen.* They're not equal yet.

T: So what do you need to do?

C: *Use more cubes in each.*

T: Go on then.

(Child continues working, adding cubes 3 at a time and 5 at a time, and discovers that 30 works.)

In this instance, which of these would deepen children's understanding more: solving the same problem in more than one way, or solving a different problem in the same way? Why?

How is this non-example supporting deeper understanding of finding common multiples?

What understanding are the cubes adding to this activity that numerals alone do not? Would a different representation, e.g. number rods, be more useful to solve this particular problem? Why?

What next?

Ask children if they can explain or show a relationship between 15 and 30 that explains why both these numbers solve the original problem. Can they find the next number that solves the problem?

Tasks in Practice

Learning task 4: Lots more and lots less

DP Year 2 > Term 3 > Unit 17 > Multiplication and division > Week 4 > Learning task 4

In this task, children find unknown multiplication facts for 5s and 10s, using multiplication facts they know.

On track

Children who are 'on track' show the number of groups increasing and how this increases the product. They link the increase in product to the size of the group each time, e.g. they show that 5 × 13 is one more lot of 5 than 5 × 12 by picking up one more train of 5 cubes.

Children have been making trains of 5 cubes to construct the 5 times table up to 5 × 12.

T: Who can tell me the answer to five times twelve?

C1: A hundred.

T: Was it? Check your working out. Five times twelve.

C1: Oh, I've only got up to eleven.

T: Who has worked out twelve lots of five?

C2: Sixty.

T: OK, so twelve groups of five would be sixty. Does that help you work out thirteen groups of five?

C1: Umm ... you have sixty, so put that in your head and add on another group.

T: How many more do you add on?

C1: Five more. The groups are five.

T: So what would the answer be?

C1: Sixty-five.

▲ This child is counting in ones. How would you support them to move on to counting in fives?

How are the trains of cubes supporting children's ability to extrapolate one multiplication fact from another?

T: Good. Who has one that we haven't done?

C2: Five times twenty.

T: What's five times twenty?

C2: It's a hundred.

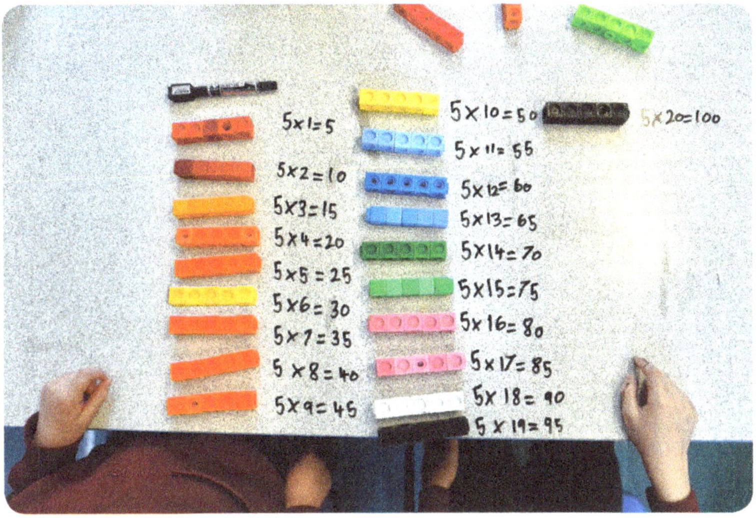

T: Right. So if we know that fact, who can tell me what twenty-one lots of five will be?

C2: It would be a hundred and five, because that one's a hundred (child points to 5 × 20 = 100), *and the next one should be five more. You add on another group of five.*

T: Good, so to find twenty-one lots of five, we take twenty lots of five and add another five, which is a hundred and five. So twenty-one lots of five is a hundred and five. Great reasoning.

Child 2 appears to have picked up clear reasoning language from Child 1. What could you say or do if this didn't happen automatically?

What next?

What is the same and what is different about 5 × 7 and 5 × 9?

Needing support

Look and listen for children who add 1 more at a time rather than one group of 5 more.

This child has written 5 × 4 + 1 = 30.

T: What are you trying to work out?

C: Five times five.

T: What do you know so far?

C: Five times four is twenty.

T: And then what's this one?

(Teacher points to 5 × 4 + 1 = 30.)

T: Five lots of four plus one?

C: Twenty-one.

T: Show me five lots of four with your cubes.

C: Five, ten, fifteen, twenty.

(Child lays out 4 trains of 5 cubes.)

(Teacher places a single cube next to the 4 lots of 5.)

T: Is this how much we should be adding, to find one more group of five? How many cubes are in each of our groups?

C: Five.

T: So what if instead of adding one, I add one more lot of five?

(Teacher replaces the single cube with another train of 5.)

C: Twenty-five.

T: Good. Do you think we need to rewrite this sentence?

C: Yes, it should be five times four plus five equals twenty-five.

(Child writes 5 × 4 + 5 = 25 below their first number sentence.)

T: Good. So is five times five (teacher shows 5 trains of 5 cubes) the same as five times four (teacher removes one train) add five?

(Teacher replaces the train.)

C: Yes!

T: Well done. If five lots of five is twenty-five, how can you work out six lots of five?

C: Five lots of five add one.

> Has this been the consequence of moving to abstract thinking too soon?

> The teacher's questioning is focusing on the meaning of the numbers in the sentence 5 × 4 + 1 = 30, not the value of the calculation. This is probing the child's understanding.

> How has the (re-)introduction of the trains of 5 cubes supported the child's abstract notation here?

(Child writes 5 × 5 + 1 = 30, and 5 × 6 = 30 above it.)

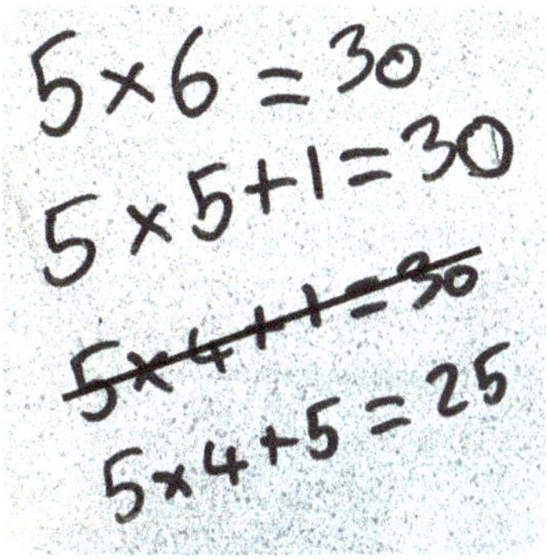

T: Hmm. Remind me what five lots of five equals?

(Teacher points to the 5 trains of 5 cubes.)

C: Twenty-five.

T: So what is twenty-five ... (teacher adds one cube) add one?

C: Twenty-six.

T: Are we meant to be adding just one? Or one group?

C: One group.

T: So, what do you think needs to change here? What were you trying to do?

C: Make it thirty.

T: Make it thirty. So, if you're trying to make it thirty, but you know five times five add one is twenty-six, what do you think you need to change?

C: Change the one to five.

T: Five! Great reasoning.

(Child alters calculation to 5 × 5 + 5 = 30.)

T: Good. You've shown that five times six is the same as five times five add five.

This is a key prompt which causes a shift in thinking by this child.

What next?

Build 5 × 3 with your trains of 5 cubes. Now show me how you would use your 5 × 3 model to get to 5 × 5. What changed and what stayed the same?

Or: starting from 5 × 10 = 50, children work out 5 × 11, 5 × 12 and 5 × 13, showing their reasoning (concrete, pictorial or abstract) each time.

Going deeper

Remind children that $5 \times 2 = 10$ and $5 \times 4 = 20$. Draw out that 20 is double 10, so 5×4 is double 5×2. Ask them to show this using cubes or a drawing, then to represent more examples as $5 \times$ ___ is double $5 \times$ ___. They can replace **double** with **half of**, **triple**, etc.

Example 1

T: How could you use the five times tables you've recorded to help you write the ten times table?

C: *Just use the equations with even numbers.*
(Child points at all the 'even' calculations of five: $5 \times 2 = 10$, $5 \times 4 = 20$, $5 \times 6 = 30$ ...)

T: So you're grouping pairs of two fives to make ten. That is amazing. OK, so rub out the others. What's your first ten times table fact going to be?

C: *Ten times one equals ten.*

T: Which of your calculations using five is equal to this?

C: *Two times five equals ten.*

T: What would the next one be in tens?

(Child records $10 \times 2 = 20$ and $2 \times 10 = 20$.)

T: And which five times table fact is this equal to?

C: *Four times five equals twenty.*

T: Good. Can you see a pattern?

C: *How many fives is going up in twos.*

T: Why is that, can you explain?

C: *A ten is two fives, so the fives go up two, four, six, and the tens go up one, two, three.*

How will you share the ways of thinking about this so that children see the same task from an alternative viewpoint?

◀ Children showing the relationship between the 5 times table and the 10 times table.

Example 2

◀ Children showing the doubling and halving patterns when working with groups of 5 and groups of 10.

T: What have you written in red? Explain to me.

(Teacher points to where child has written 1 × 5 = 5 in red, above 2 × 5 = 10.)

C: *So it's half of the black number. You halve it and it gives you the red number.*

T: Yes, if we're looking at the answers. So one times five is five and one times ten is ten, isn't it? What was interesting about that?

C: *Five is half of ten.*

T: What else could you say?

C: *You could say that half of ten is five and half of twenty is ten and half of thirty is fifteen and half of forty is twenty.*

T: So, if I hid this (teacher covers 5 × 5 = 25 leaving 10 × 5 = 50 showing), you would know what five times five is?

C: *Yes.*

T: Using that halving, can you tell me what five times five is?

C: *Twenty-five.*

T: Because ...?

C: *Because if you halve fifty you get twenty-five.*

What rule can you write about the relationship between 5 × a number and 10 × a number?

What next?

10 × ☐ = 5 × ☐

How many ways could you make this true?

Chapter 4
Fractions

Strand overview

Aims

Children develop fluency with dividing objects, groups and quantities into halves, quarters and thirds. They find fractions in concrete contexts to secure 'whole-to-part' fluency and scale up (e.g. from one-quarter to multiple quarters) to develop 'part-to-whole' fluency. They reason about calculations such as $\frac{1}{2}$ of 6 = 3 using concrete wholes, e.g. $\frac{1}{2}$ of 6 m is 3 m, and justify the equivalence of two fractions such as $\frac{2}{4} = \frac{1}{2}$, e.g. $\frac{2}{4}$ of 100 ml is equal to $\frac{1}{2}$ of 100 ml. They solve problems using a given fraction of a whole to find another fraction of the same whole and compare fractional parts when wholes are equal and unequal.

Key ideas

- Children move away from sharing in ones. When finding a quarter of 8 objects, they should prepare 4 'parts' and put 2 objects in each, rather than sharing them out one at a time.
- Practical experiences prepare children for the abstract concepts: 'fraction of' as an operation, e.g. $\frac{1}{2}$ of 8 is 4; and representing fractions on a number line.
- The number $\frac{1}{4}$ is $\frac{1}{4}$ of what? The number line explains that $\frac{1}{4}$ is the endpoint of a journey $\frac{1}{4}$ of the way between 0 and 1.
- The numbers $\frac{1}{2}$ and $\frac{2}{4}$ are equal, but the proportions $\frac{1}{2}$ of ... and $\frac{2}{4}$ of ... may or may not be equal, e.g. $\frac{1}{2}$ of a grape is not the same amount of fruit as $\frac{2}{4}$ of a watermelon.

Models and apparatus

Children need to halve, third and quarter in many different practical contexts, e.g. cut a length of ribbon in half, divide a jug of juice into thirds. Fractions should continue to be represented concretely, e.g. using number rods, alongside abstract representations on a number line.

View the video on the Year 2 Teacher Support area of the Digital Planner

Progression through the National Curriculum

Year 1

- Recognize, find and name a half as one of two equal parts of an object, shape or quantity.
- Recognize, find and name a quarter as one of four equal parts of an object, shape or quantity.

Year 2

- Recognize, find, name and write fractions $\frac{1}{3}$, $\frac{1}{4}$, $\frac{2}{4}$ and $\frac{3}{4}$ of a length, shape, set of objects or quantity.
- Write simple fractions for example, $\frac{1}{2}$ of 6 = 3 and recognize the equivalence of $\frac{2}{4}$ and $\frac{1}{2}$.

Year 3

- Count up and down in tenths; recognize that tenths arise from dividing an object into 10 equal parts and in dividing 1-digit numbers or quantities by 10.
- Recognize, find and write fractions of a discrete set of objects: unit fractions and non-unit fractions with small denominators.
- Recognize and use fractions as numbers: unit fractions and non-unit fractions with small denominators.
- Recognize and show, using diagrams, equivalent fractions with small denominators.
- Add and subtract fractions with the same denominator within one whole (for example, $\frac{5}{7} + \frac{1}{7} = \frac{6}{7}$).
- Compare and order unit fractions, and fractions with the same denominators.
- Solve problems that involve all of the above.

Year 2 sub-objectives

Term 1

- Recognize, find, name and write fractions $\frac{1}{4}$, $\frac{2}{4}$ and $\frac{3}{4}$ of a length, shape, set of objects or quantity.
- Write simple fractions, for example $\frac{1}{2}$ of 6 = 3.

Term 2

- Recognize, find, name and write fractions $\frac{1}{3}$, $\frac{1}{4}$, $\frac{2}{4}$ and $\frac{3}{4}$ of a length, shape, set of objects or quantity.
- Write simple fractions, for example $\frac{1}{2}$ of 6 = 3, and recognize the equivalence of $\frac{2}{4}$ and $\frac{1}{2}$.

Term 3

- Recognize, find, name and write fractions $\frac{1}{3}$, $\frac{1}{4}$, $\frac{2}{4}$ and $\frac{3}{4}$ of a length, set of objects or quantity.
- Write simple fractions, for example $\frac{1}{2}$ of 6 = 3, and recognize the equivalence of $\frac{2}{4}$ and $\frac{1}{2}$.

Tasks in Practice

Launch task: Fraction picnic

DP Year 2 > Term 1 > Unit 5 > Fractions > Week 9 > Launch task

In this task, children share a picnic into two and then four equal parts, to get practical experience of halving and quartering a collection of objects.

On track

Children who are 'on track' show picnic items correctly halved and shared between two people: a 'group' item (cookies), a 'one' item (cake) and a 'continuous' item (drink).

Children have been asked to share the following picnic items equally between two people: a bottle of water, 12 cookies, 2 apples, 4 sandwiches and 1 cake. (Teacher created their own images to cut out, including a cake with chocolate icing and a cherry on top.)

T: How many apples on each plate?

C: One!

T: One, good. And how much cake on each plate?

C: Half.

T: Oh, well done. Why did you do that to the cake?

C1: Because it's equal.

C2: Because it was one whole.

T: So it was one whole and what did you do to the cake?

C: We cut it in half because ... to make it equal.

T: Super, to make it equal. Why did you cut it this way and not the other way?

(Teacher gestures to show that the child cut the cake vertically down the centre, rather than horizontally.)

C: Because it's going to be in half. Otherwise you won't have half the cherry or half the icing.

T: Super answer, really clear explaining. Well done.

The teacher explains what they are praising; namely, the reasoning as well as the answer.

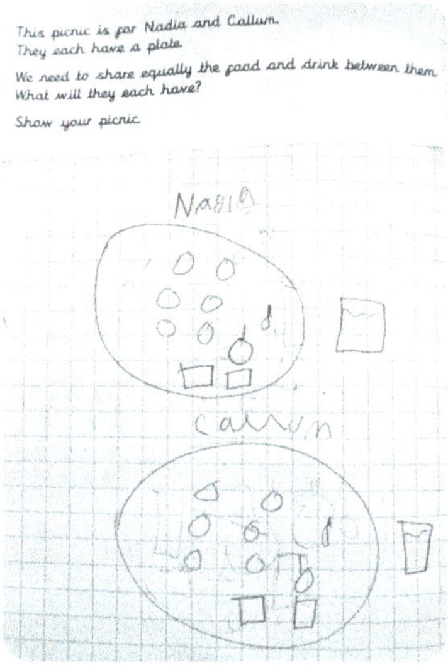

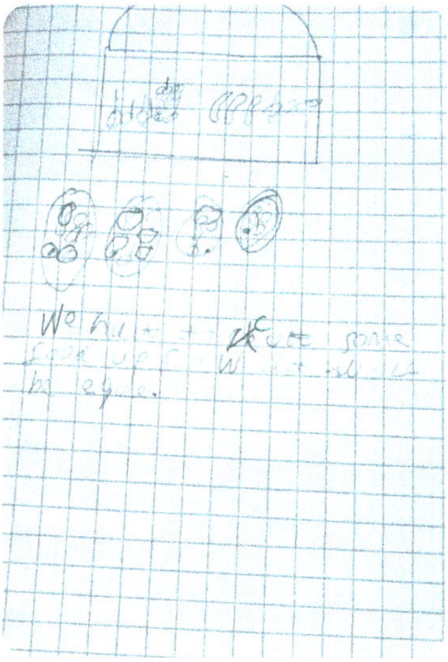

What kind of recording will you expect from your children? How will you ensure it shows halves and quarters as equal parts/quantities?

◀ 'We had to cut some food up so it will be equal'.

What next?

Children share a continuous quantity (a drink) equally between two identical cups. Support them in adjusting the amounts so they are visually equal. How could they check if they have been accurate?

▲ How can we make sure the drink is shared equally between two?

Did anyone find halves of the bottle of drink in a different way?

Needing support

Look and listen for children who try to share discrete quantities as though they were continuous (e.g. measuring the cookies rather than counting them) or vice versa (e.g. counting out 'shares' of juice rather than measuring the depth in each cup), and those who create (and don't then adjust) unequal sharing.

This child has not cut the cake in half equally: the cut is off-centre.

The teacher carefully questions to work out if the child knows that the parts should be equal but doesn't have the dexterity to make them so, or if the child doesn't know that they should be equal.

T: Have you cut it exactly in half?

C: No.

T: What should you have done?

C: Cut down the middle of the cherry?

T: Here's another cake. Do you think you can cut it exactly in half? How could you do that?

C: Um ... draw a line?

T: OK.

C: And then fold it.

T: Good idea. Will you fold this in half please?

(Child folds the cake, not quite in half.)

T: So I'll have this piece (teacher points to the bigger side) and you get that piece (teacher points to the smaller side).

C: Ohh ...

Do two halves have to 'match'?

T: What's the problem?

C: These aren't equal. This is bigger.

T: Try again to fold it.

(Child folds carefully.)

C: Now each person gets the same.

T: OK, you can cut now. Make sure it's equal. Would they each get a cherry?

C: No. Is it half a cherry?

T: Good. They both get half a cherry.

How does insisting on precision around halving support this child's learning?

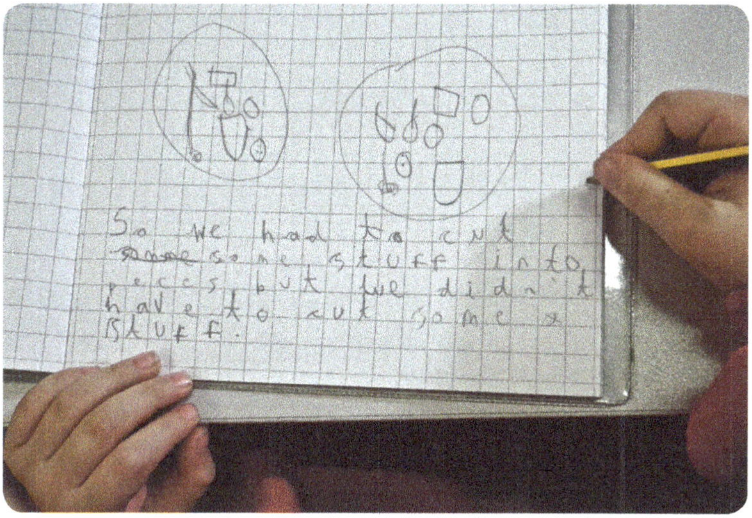

▲ A child's recording: We had to cut some stuff into pieces but we didn't have to cut some stuff.

How can you support children to use mathematical language in their recording?

What next?

Ask children how we can share the drink equally between two people.

Going deeper

Two more friends arrive and the children decide to share the picnic equally. What will each friend get on their plate?

▲ Here children are working practically to work out the fractions for the additional guests.

T: How did you change the sharing of the cake when the extra guests arrived?

C: Cut it in four pieces!

T: Good. So explain what you did the first time with the cake?

C: We cut it in two parts. So, half the cake over here, and there was half the cake for this person. So we can give one each to the first person and the second person.

T: So when I put them both together, what kind of cake is this?

C: A whole.

T: And the first time you did a cut down the middle and you cut it in ...?

C: Half.

T: What does that mean? How many equal parts do you have?

C: Two equal parts.

How would you respond if children started from the beginning again (by putting all of the picnic back together) and then shared into quarters, rather than adjusting the halves to make quarters?

T: Super. And then when you had four people what did you do next?

C: Cut it in half another time.

T: Show me.

(Child carefully cuts one half cake in half again.)

T: So, you have to cut half a cake in half again. Do you agree?

C1: Yes!

C2: You have to put it in a quarter.

T: Excellent! What was that word?

C: A quarter.

T: A quarter, what does that mean?

C: When you have half and then you cut it down the middle.

T: So, when you cut the cake in half you got two parts. But then you had to cut the half in half again, and when you cut the half in half you got two parts. Do you agree?

C: Yes.

T: So how many equal parts did you make altogether?

C: Four.

T: Four what?

C: Four equal parts.

T: And what's the word we use?

C: Quarter. Each part is one-quarter.

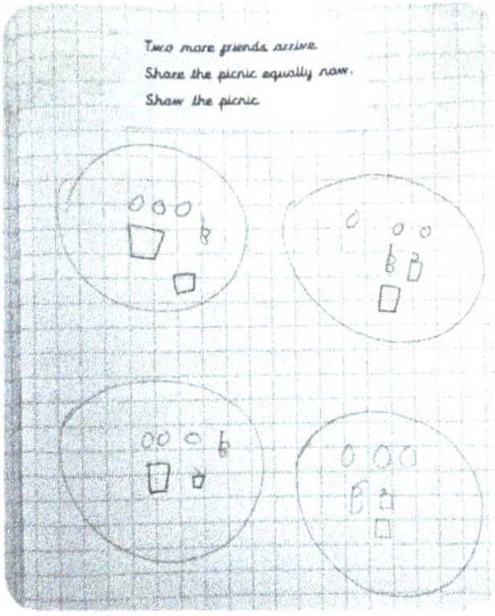

How is this task preparing children for the idea of equivalence with fractions?

This language could be shared with the whole class.

What next?

Children show two different ways of sharing two apples between four people.

Tasks in Practice

Learning task 5: Comparing fraction lengths

DP Year 2 > Term 2 > Unit 12 > Fractions > Week 8 > Learning task 5

In this task, children compare fractional lengths, relative to each other and then to a known length.

On track

Children who are 'on track' express one length as a multiple of another, and the second length as a fraction of the first. They can use the fractional relationships between unknown lengths and a 1 metre length to work out the unknowns.

Children have been given four ribbons: $1\frac{3}{4}$ m, $1\frac{1}{2}$ m, $\frac{3}{4}$ m and $\frac{1}{2}$ m. They do not know the lengths. They have also been given a black ribbon that they know is 1 metre. They need to find the length of the $1\frac{1}{2}$ metre (pale blue) ribbon.

T: How can we find the length of this ribbon?

(Teacher points to blue ribbon.)

C1: *We can measure it with this one* (child points to the black ribbon). *It's one metre.*

T: And that's the only one we know for certain, isn't it? So we need to use it to measure.

(Children place the black ribbon against the blue ribbon on the floor to measure 1 metre.)

T: That takes us to here.

(Child 1 puts a finger at the 1 metre point.)

C1: *It's one metre and a half!*

T: How can you check that?

C1: *I'll keep my finger here on the blue ribbon. You check it with the black metre ribbon.*

C2: *I'll fold it in half.*

How many different lengths could you use the 1 metre ribbon to check? How would you do this?

(Child 2 folds the 1 metre ribbon in half.)

T: Good, we can fold it in half. So how long is the black ribbon now? How many equal parts are there?

C2: There are two equal parts so it's half a metre. We could use this to measure the blue ribbon instead.

(Children measure using the folded black ribbon – now half a metre – finding that it fits along the blue ribbon 3 times.)

Some children will find the coordination and dexterity aspects of this task hard. How would you support them so they can still engage successfully with this task?

▲ Children fold the black 1 m ribbon in half (now $\frac{1}{2}$ m) to measure the $1\frac{1}{2}$ m blue ribbon.

C1: The folded black ribbon fits three times, so the blue ribbon is ... half a metre ... one metre ... one and a half metres.

(Child counts the length in half metres.)

What fraction of the blue ribbon is the black ribbon?

What next?

Ask children to fold the black ribbon in half again (to make $\frac{1}{4}$ m). What length does this make? Which of the ribbons can you use it to measure?

Needing support

Look and listen for children only making direct comparisons (e.g. *This is longer than that*) or very approximate multiplicative comparisons (e.g. guessing that any longer piece is twice as long as a shorter piece).

The teacher shows the child a black $1\frac{1}{2}$ m ribbon and a dark pink $\frac{1}{2}$ m ribbon.

T: Can you compare the lengths of these two ribbons?

C: This one's longer.

(Child points to the black $1\frac{1}{2}$ m ribbon.)

T: OK.

(Teacher adds another $\frac{1}{2}$ m ribbon to the first $\frac{1}{2}$ m ribbon to make 1 m.)

T: Which one is longer now? Can you tell me?

C: I'm picking this one.

(Child points to the black $1\frac{1}{2}$ m ribbon.)

(Teacher adds another $\frac{1}{2}$ m ribbon to the first two $\frac{1}{2}$ m ribbons to make $1\frac{1}{2}$ m.)

At what point should you intervene when children only make direct comparisons of the two lengths?

T: Which one is longer now?

C: They're the same.

(Teacher points to the black $1\frac{1}{2}$ m ribbon.)

T: So if I call this the whole, what can you tell me about these parts?

C: There are three of them.

T: And what can you tell me about the lengths of these three ribbons?

C: They're all the same.

T: That's right – I have split one whole into three equal parts. What fraction is each part?

C: One-third?

T: Good. Tell me a sentence about the length of the pink ribbon compared to the length of the black one.

C: The pink one is one-third of the length of the black one.

Why does the teacher ask this question when an answer of one-third has already been provided?

How has this child's comparative thinking moved on through teacher intervention?

What next?

Can you find me two ribbons where the shorter ribbon is one half of the longer ribbon?

Going deeper

Show the $1\frac{1}{2}$ m length. Ask: *What is this half of?* Then ask children to work out what it is $\frac{1}{3}$ of, and the same for another length, e.g. $1\frac{3}{4}$ m.

The teacher points to the black $1\frac{1}{2}$ m ribbon on the left.

T: We want to know what this black ribbon is one half of.

C: *We need to have two of them. This one looks like it might be the same length.*

(Child measures a pale blue ribbon against the black one to check their lengths are equal, and then lines up the blue ribbon at the end of the black one. Child points to the 1 m black ribbon on the right.)

C: *That's one metre.*

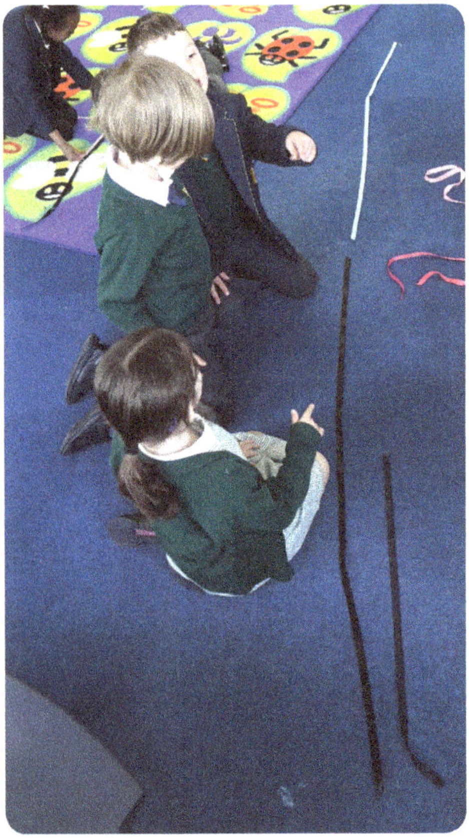

How does this task provide opportunities to think about different fractional relationships?

Why is it important that children work from the fractional part to find the whole?

Do the small procedural mistakes here (e.g. that the ribbons aren't straight and they don't join up) matter? Do they undermine the subsequent reasoning?

T: So, if we want to measure that whole length, and we know that this ribbon is one metre, how can we do that?

C: Let's see how many times the one metre goes into the whole length.

(Child uses 1 metre ribbon as a benchmark, and finds that it fits into the whole length three times.)

T: So, how many times did the metre go into the whole lot?

C: Three times.

T: Ah, so how could you explain that as a fraction of the whole length?

C: It is a third.

T: Tell me what you know about the ribbons.

C: So, we know that the black measuring ribbon is one metre, and it's a third of the whole length, so it's three metres.

T: Can you use a full sentence?

C: The whole is three metres and the longer black ribbon is one-half of that whole.

What next?

Children calculate the original length ($1\frac{1}{2}$ m), before working out, using ribbons, what it is $\frac{1}{3}$ of and $\frac{1}{4}$ of.

Tasks in Practice

Learning task 1: Starting fractions

DP Year 2 > Term 3 > Unit 20 > Fractions > Week 7 > Learning task 1

In this task, children use a given fraction of a continuous whole to find another fraction of the same whole.

On track

Children who are 'on track' use fractional parts and their relationship to the whole to create related proportions, e.g. knowing that two-thirds can be halved to find one-third, then using this to find the whole, which is three-thirds.

Children have been shown this problem:

- A shop sells full lengths, half lengths and three-quarter lengths of ribbon. Nadia is buying some ribbon for an art project. She needs a piece at least 20 cm long. She can see that the half length is 12 cm. Can she use this information to work out whether a three-quarter length would be long enough?

The teacher and children have agreed to use string to represent the ribbon.

C: *This piece of string is already half and it is twelve centimetres. And we're going to cut the other piece of string in half again so it's six centimetres.*

T: Why are you going to cut it so it's six centimetres?

C: *Because then we've got the right amount of string to see if it's long enough for her project. We need a three-quarter length and we have a half length. And when you cut a half length in half it becomes a quarter length. Half is equal to two quarters.*

T: Brilliant, can you show me what you're going to do with the string to check?

▲ Can you cut your string in half without measuring on the ruler? How?

Could children still solve this problem with unknown lengths of ribbon?

How precisely are children communicating relationships between quarters, halves and wholes?

(Child places the 12 cm piece and the 6 cm piece against the ruler and measures 18 cm.)

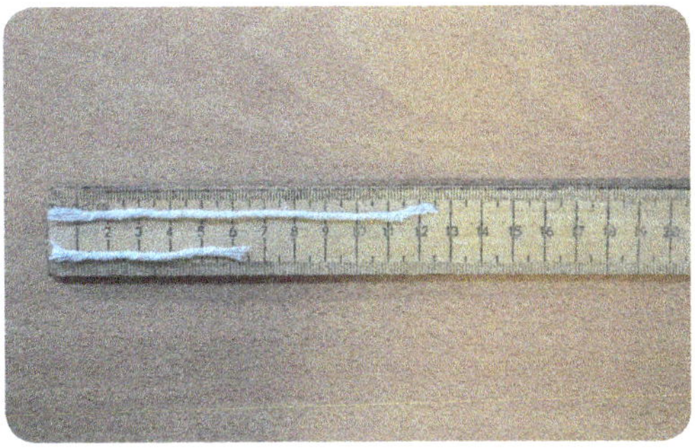

▲ What can you say about your two pieces of string?

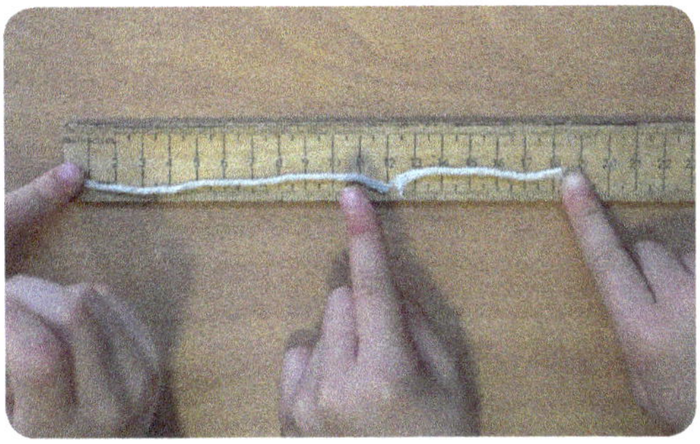

▲ How long would a full length of string be?

C: *That's twelve centimetres and this one is six centimetres, and together they are eighteen centimetres which is a half and quarter added together to make three-quarters.*

T: Will a three-quarter length be long enough for Nadia's project?

C: *No, it's too short. It's eighteen centimetres and she needs twenty centimetres.*

T: Well done, good reasoning.

Are a quarter and a half always equal to three-quarters, even when the whole length of ribbon is different?

What next?

Select children to share their thinking and methods with the class. What is the same and what is different? E.g. some children may have found a quarter and added it to a half; some may have added three lots of one-quarter.

What generalizations are children making? Here we can check if children are generalizing that a half plus a quarter is always equal to three quarters.

Needing support

Look and listen for children attempting to cut the half length of ribbon into four equal parts to find one-quarter.

Children have been cutting their half length of string into 3 or 4 pieces. The teacher uses cubes to model the problem and address misunderstanding. He holds up a train of 4 interlocking cubes.

▲ Four cubes is half the amount. Eight cubes is the whole amount.

In the problem, are we asked to find three-quarters of half of the ribbon, or three-quarters of the whole ribbon? Listen to hear children's responses.

T: This is half of your ribbon. If I give you another half (teacher gives children another train of 4 cubes) you now have a whole ribbon. This is your whole, can you find three-quarters of that? If you need to find three-quarters, how many equal groups?

C: *Four.*

T: Go on then.

(Children break their cubes into 4 equal groups of 2 cubes.)

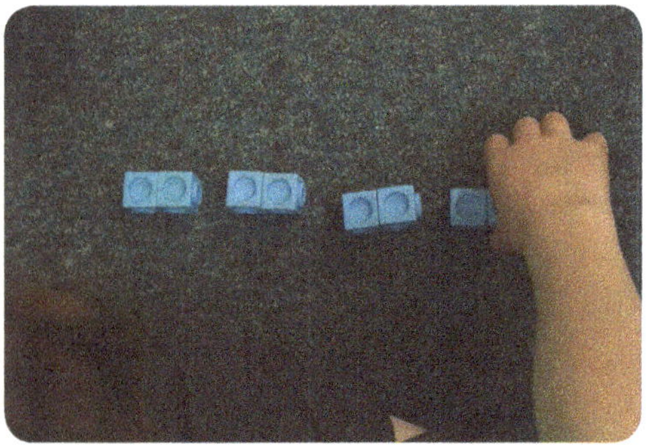

▲ Divide the whole (eight cubes) into quarters.

Show me the cubes that represent half. Now show me three of the quarters. How many more quarters is three-quarters than half? How many fewer quarters is three-quarters than the whole? Check children can show you the one-quarter more and one-quarter less here.

T: How many of the four equal parts do we want? Look at the fraction.

C: Three.

T: Yes. We want three-quarters. So, join the three quarters together.

(Children join 3 of their groups of 2 cubes together.)

T: Good, so a half piece of ribbon was four cubes, and a three-quarter piece of ribbon is ...?

C: Six cubes.

T: Well done.

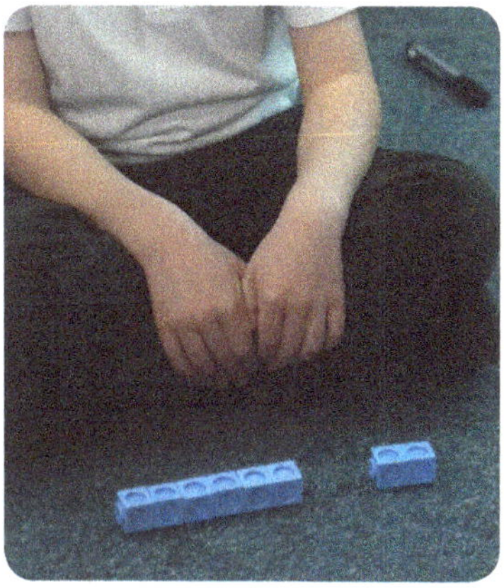

▲ This is three-quarters.

What next?

Children move back to working with ribbon but keep the cubes available. As you work with the ribbon alongside children, use sentence frames to emphasize the relationships between three-quarters, quarter, half and the whole. E.g.:

Here is half of the ribbon.

Half is equal to ___ quarters.

A quarter is half of a ___.

Three-quarters is ___ (one) more quarter than the ___ (half) length of the ribbon.

Three-quarters is ___ (one) less quarter than the____ (whole) length of the ribbon.

Three-quarters is ___ (three) lots of ___ (one-quarter).

When children return to the ribbon, how would you ensure that their understanding of the three-quarters relationship with the whole and half is transferred to the real-life context?

Going deeper

Ask children to explain why dividing two-thirds into two equal amounts helped them to solve a sandcastle problem.

Children have been shown this problem:

- Dev made a sandcastle. But the sea washed one-third of it away. Yasmin wants to build a sandcastle using the same amount of sand as Dev. How can she use the sand that is left in Dev's sandcastle to find out how much he used altogether?

Children were given 200 ml of sand, and were told it was two-thirds of the total amount used for Dev's sandcastle. They were asked to find the whole amount used.

C: *It's three hundred.*

T: **Why do you need to get to three hundred? I agree, but why?**

C: *That's going to be three-thirds if two hundred is two-thirds.*

T: **Why is that? What do you need to do first?**

C: *So, we halved two hundred to get one hundred.*

This questioning is developing the habit of always giving full reasoning. High-attaining children often want to give you just the answer and move on to the next question, so they can 'get another one right'.

T: **Why have you halved two hundred?**

C: *Because we wanted to find one-third. And then we times it by three.*

T: **Why did you times it by three?**

C1: Because we wanted to find three-thirds.

C2: Yes, or we could do two hundred add one hundred.

T: So, you halved two-thirds to find one-third. Then you multiplied one-third by three to get three-thirds. Or you could add two-thirds to one-third to make three-thirds. Well done. So, if two-thirds is two hundred millilitres of sand, how much sand is three-thirds?

C: Three hundred millilitres.

T: Good job.

Is this the same approach children used for finding three-quarters of the ribbon, or are they trying out different approaches?

Will your method for finding three-thirds of the sand when two-thirds is known work for any amount of sand?

What next?

Show me two more ways of finding three-thirds of *any* amount when you know two-thirds of it. Or two more ways of finding three-quarters of an amount when you know half of it.

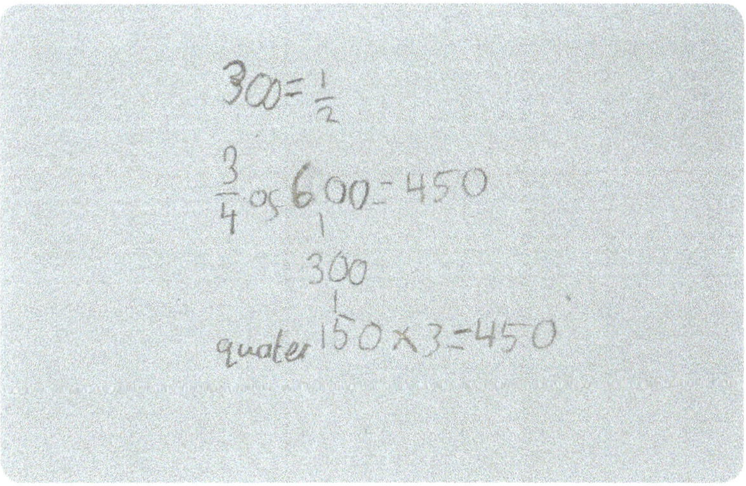

▲ Children find the three-quarter amount of sand, when the half amount is 300 ml.

What pictorial representation would support the numerical reasoning shown here?

Chapter 5
Statistics

Strand overview

Aims

Children solve problems that require them to gather information from and about people, such as finding out what sandwiches to make for a class picnic through a survey of each child's favourite sandwich filling. They reason about, and draw inferences from, the data they collect. They become fluent with making predictions and posing hypotheses; carrying out simple surveys; displaying relevant data using tally charts, data tables, pictograms and block diagrams (not only 1 : 1 scales); interpreting the representations and drawing conclusions that relate to the original problem. These conclusions might be qualitative (e.g. Lots more children chose cheese than jam), additive (e.g. 10 more children chose cheese than jam), or multiplicative (e.g. Twice as many children chose cheese as jam).

Key ideas

- Be alert to: children forgetting the source of the data, e.g. forgetting that each cube in a block graph records an actual response, and hence making conclusions about the numbers of blocks not the numbers of people; and not detaching themselves from the data: e.g. thinking that a survey of a class's 'favourite sandwich' is a survey of their class.
- All the information in a data representation conveys meaning including the title, key and labels.
- The data that are gathered can restrict the scope of the conclusions that can be drawn from them. Survey questions and data collection methods need to be carefully designed so that justifiable conclusions can be drawn.

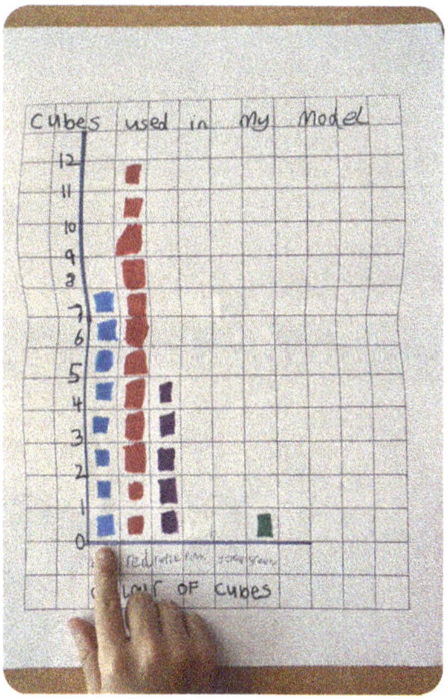

Models and apparatus

Children should make cube towers and sticker charts before drawing block diagrams and pictograms, to reinforce the connection between data collection and data representation: a drawn shape represents a real token which represents an actual person. They should become fluent with using tally charts to record data that occur quickly (e.g. the colours of passing cars), or over an extended period of time (e.g. school lunch choices over a half-term).

View the video on the Year 2 Teacher Support area of the Digital Planner

Progression through the National Curriculum

Year 1

- *No Year 1 objectives for this strand.*

Year 2

- Interpret and construct simple pictograms, tally charts, block diagrams and simple tables.
- Ask and answer simple questions by counting the number of objects in each category and sorting the categories by quantity.
- Ask and answer questions about totalling and comparing categorical data.

Year 3

- Interpret and present data using bar charts, pictograms and tables.
- Solve one-step and two-step questions (for example, 'How many more?' and 'How many fewer?') using information presented in scaled bar charts and pictograms and tables.

Year 2 sub-objectives

Term 2

- Interpret and construct simple pictograms and block diagrams.
- Ask and answer simple questions by counting the number of objects in each category.
- Ask and answer questions about categorical data.

Term 3

- Interpret and construct simple pictograms, tally charts, block diagrams and simple tables.
- Ask and answer simple questions by counting the number of objects in each category and sorting the categories by quantity.
- Ask and answer questions about totalling and comparing categorical data.

Tasks in Practice

Learning task 2: It's all about us

DP Year 2 > Term 2 > Unit 10 > Statistics > Week 5 > Learning task 2

In this task, children undertake simple surveys about likes in the class and then represent the collected data in a block diagram.

On track

Children who are 'on track' explain how their diagrams show the results of their surveys, and what the diagrams show about the class's preferences.

Children selected four well-known books, and made predictions about the relative popularity of each one. They asked the class to vote on their favourite. Children drew a block diagram to show the results.

T: What does your data show?

C1: Stick Man got fourteen. Love Monster got none.

C2: The Gruffalo got two and The Gruffalo's Child got six.

T: Going back to your predictions, were there any that were wrong?

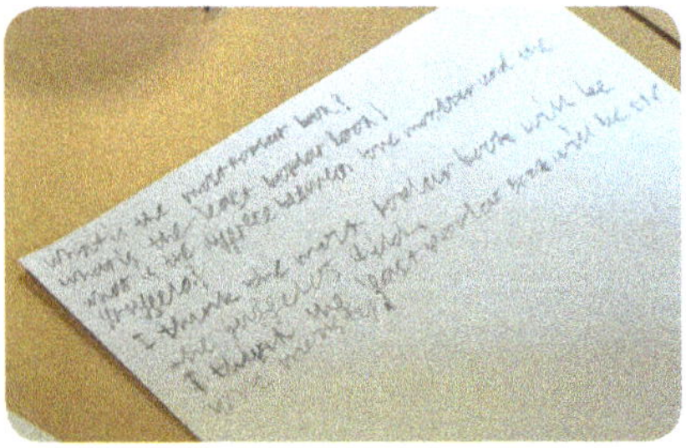

◀ A child's predictions: I think the most popular book will be The Gruffalo's Child. I think the least popular book will be Love Monster.

C2: We said that The Gruffalo's Child would be the most.

T: Has that come up as the most popular?

How can you give children opportunities to demonstrate their understanding of the language, and to reflect on their predictions?

C1: No, Stick Man was the most, it was fourteen.

◀ Children have added two extra blocks onto the side of their diagram to represent 14 votes for Stick Man.

T: So, The Gruffalo's Child was less popular than you expected?

C2: We thought it would be most, but it's the second most.

T: Did that surprise you with Love Monster? Have you completed that bit or did no one vote for it?

C2: We thought it would be the least popular, and it was.

T: How many people voted for it?

C1: None.

T: What's your question on difference?

C2: What is the difference between Love Monster and The Gruffalo?

T: Are you able to answer that now, looking at your data? What's the difference between how many people chose Love Monster and how many chose The Gruffalo as their favourite book?

C2: Two.

T: Full sentence please.

C2: Two more people chose The Gruffalo than Love Monster. The difference between them is two votes.

T: Good sentences.

Do you always have to represent all the results in your diagram, even if one of the choices got zero votes?

How did you work out what the difference is?

What next?

Children record a final list of statements that their diagram represents, then exchange them with another group. They read the statements and look at the diagram. Do they agree or disagree? Can they think of another statement?

Needing support

Look and listen for children who do not make the connection between the survey and the diagrams, e.g. they do not say that the tallest column shows the most popular choice in each category. Also look and listen for children who are not coming up with statements about their diagram.

T: In your survey of favourite fruit, I think some children chose grapes. Do you agree?

C: *Yes.*

T: How do you know?

C: *They put a cube in this cup.*

T: How many did? Let's make a tower with the cubes.

(Child connects all the cubes from the cup then counts them.)

C: *Eleven.*

T: What does eleven cubes tell us?

C: *How many children liked grapes.*

T: Yes, how many is that?

C: *Eleven.*

T: Let's write a sentence. What can we say?

C: *They liked grapes.*

T: Did everyone? Or do we know a number?

C: *Eleven.*

T: Full sentence please.

C: *Eleven liked grapes.*

T: Did they just like it? Or was it their favourite?

C: *Favourite.*

T: Yes. Eleven children said grapes were their favourite fruit. Do you agree?

C: *Yes!*

T: Now you say the sentence.

C: *Eleven children said grapes were their favourite fruit.*

How can you guide children gently through the thinking process they will need to use when working independently?

How does saying the complete sentence themselves help children to take ownership of the information?

T: Can you colour the right number of squares on the block diagram, to show this?

(Child colours 11 squares in the first column of the diagram.)

T: Good. How many chose peaches as their favourite? Let's make a tower.

(Child does so and counts the cubes.)

C: *Four did.*

T: Tell me that in a sentence.

C: *Four children said peaches were their favourite fruit.*

(Teacher lies the grapes and peaches towers next to each other.)

T: Look at these towers next to each other. Is the grapes tower taller or shorter?

C: *Much taller. Eleven is more than four.*

T: How many squares will you colour to show the peaches tower?

C: *Four squares.*

(Child starts colouring up to the 5 mark.)

T: Is that right? How many squares are you colouring?

C: *Oh, I've gone a bit too far.*

(Child completes the column correctly.)

T: So which fruit did more children say was their favourite, grapes or peaches?

C: *Grapes.*

T: How do you know?

C: *I coloured in more squares. Eleven is more than four.*

T: Shall we add some labels so you don't forget what these represent?

What has the teacher done up to this point that has led to the child offering, unaided, a complete sentence articulating the meaning of part of the diagram?

▲ The side-by-side comparison reinforces the transference of meaning from the data collection (the cubes in the cups) to the data representation (the block graph).

What next?

Ask children who are not making connections between the survey and diagrams to work backwards from their chart, using prompts, e.g. How did you know you needed to shade in this square on the chart?

Going deeper

If you have two or more classes in a year group, children can compare and contrast their class's outcomes with another class's. Otherwise, survey another class in school and use their data. *Why might they be the same or different?*

T: So, your question was 'what is your favourite colour?' If you asked a different group of people, would you change your choices, or would you keep them the same?

C: I don't know. If I was asking adults, I think I'd change the colours.

T: Why?

C: Because they probably like colours that children don't really know.

This child is demonstrating an ability to step back from the immediate context and demonstrate some mature reasoning, using what they know/interpret from their own experiences.

T: Interesting. OK, and if you asked a different class in the school and kept them the same colours do you think you'd get different results?

C: Maybe, but it matters what they like.

T: Do you think there'll be much of a difference?

C: Not really. Because, if you have a colour, it's the same colour, so it just matters about what they like. But, it's rare to have adults and children have exactly the same results so I think it would be a bit different if we asked adults instead.

T: What was your most popular colour for children?

C: Red.

T: Do you think if you asked adults it would still be red? Or a different colour?

C: I think it would be black. I'd add that colour to my list.

T: Why is that?

C: A lot of grown ups wear black clothes a lot of the time, and not so many children do.

T: OK. Now let's imagine you were asking a different group of children. Can you take some cubes and put them on top of the bars on your diagram to show us what you think the differences might be? How many cubes do you think you should use?

C: *The same number as the number of children we asked in our class, to make it fair.*

(Child count out the right number of cubes, then decides how to share them amongst the six colours. He assumes a similar pattern but with small variations.)

T: Which colour have you imagined is the favourite?

C: *I've picked blue this time because it is my favourite and it was the second choice in our class.*

The idea of a 'fair' survey could be discussed with the whole class.

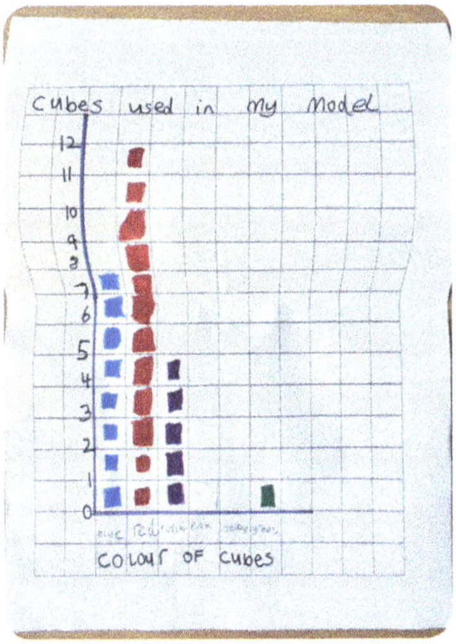

What next?

Children carry out a small survey with some adults (e.g. parents/carers and neighbours); they agree with them which colours to survey first. They compare their results to their class survey. Were their predictions on what would be the same and different correct?

Tasks in Practice

Learning task 2: Block diagram detectives

DP Year 2 > Term 3 > Unit 19 > Statistics > Week 6 > Learning task 2

In this task, children read, interpret and devise questions about a block diagram at different stages of its completion.

On track

Children who are 'on track' 'read' information from a partial diagram and make key statements about what it shows (and does not show). They talk about the different parts of the diagram that give information (labels, scale, title and bars).

Children are shown a completed block diagram titled 'Eggs laid by Farmer Yolk's hens in August' and asked to think of a question that can be answered by looking at the diagram.

T: Who has a good mathematical question that they can ask using this data – this information – here?

C: How many eggs do the chickens lay in a month?

T: Can I work that out by looking at it?

▲ Child's question: How many eggs do the chickens lay in a month?

C: Yes.

T: How do I work that out?

Can you provide opportunities for children to demonstrate and justify how their question can be answered using the diagram?

C: We've worked it out already –altogether it made a hundred and three.

T: A hundred and three? How did you find the total?

C: We counted each block of two, then we counted on one at the end because Diddy has an odd number.

T: I see, you counted in twos. How do you know each block is two eggs?

C: Because it goes up in twos.

T: Yes, we can see on the scale that each block is two, well done. Is there another way you could add them all up?

C: We could add up the number of eggs each chicken laid.

T: OK. You could record the number of eggs for each chicken and then add the numbers. So, for example, Yolky laid twenty-four and Cluckie laid ...?

C: Fourteen.

T: Good. So what would your statement be about the total number of eggs?

C: Altogether the chickens laid one hundred and three eggs.

T: Great. Who laid the most eggs?

C: Yolky laid the most eggs.

▲ A child's question: How many less eggs does Dippy have than Yolky?

How will you embed the correct mathematical language for children?

When and why is it beneficial to encourage children to confirm their answers using a complete sentence?

How many more eggs did Yolky lay than the chicken who laid the fewest eggs?

Children could use base-10 apparatus to represent each hen's total, and then amalgamate them, with regrouping, to work out the total.

What next?

Pairs write four statements about the data. Share as a class and agree whether each statement is true or not.

Needing support

Look and listen for children who are very limited in the observations they make about the diagram, and do not devise appropriate questions or who only make one statement about the completed diagram. Also look and listen for children providing disconnected evidence for their statements, e.g. *The short one was 4.*

Children have been asked to think of a question that can be answered by reading the diagram.

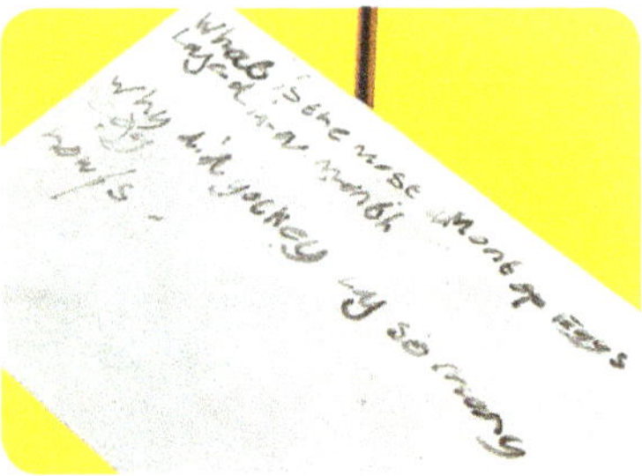

◀ A child's question: Why did Yolky lay so many eggs?

C: *Why did Yolky lay so many eggs?*

T: It's a good question, but I can't answer it with the information. Think of a 'how many' question.

C: *How many eggs has Cluckie laid?*

T: Great question. How many eggs did Cluckie lay? Can you find the answer on the graph?

(Child points to Cluckie's bar.)

T: Good. So how many eggs did Cluckie lay?

C: *Fourteen.*

T: Good. Now, can you write a statement comparing two of the chickens? Comparing the amount they laid?

C: *Umm ...*

T: Let's look at Dippy's bar, and ... which other chicken's bar shall we look at?

C: *Yolky.*

T: Okay, Dippy and Yolky. Did they lay the same amount of eggs?

C: *No.*

It may be helpful to record this (unanswerable) question and return to it later in the lesson and ask: *Can we answer this question using the diagram? Why/why not?*

How can sentence stems be used to guide children's thinking? Could this help them ask a question?

In what ways is it helpful to prompt children to answer their own question?

T: No? Who laid more eggs?

C: Yolky.

T: How do you know that?

C: The bar is longer.

(Child points at Yolky's bar.)

T: Good. What could you say to compare Yolky's and Dippy's numbers of eggs?

C: Yolky's bar is longer than Dippy's?

T: That's good, but let's talk about the amount of eggs. Could I say Yolky laid fewer eggs than Dippy?

C: No!

T: No? What should I say?

C: More.

T: Can you say it in a full sentence? Yolky laid ...

C: Yolky laid more eggs than Dippy.

T: That's great. Can you work out how many more eggs Yolky laid than Dippy?

The teacher checks that the child understands the meaning of the block graph.

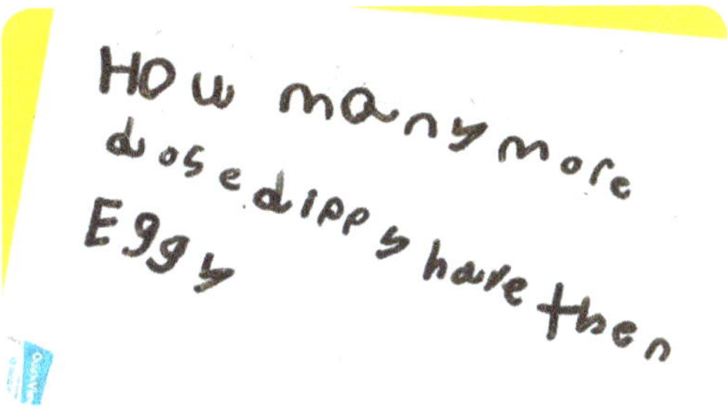

▲ This child has devised only one question and cannot think of a second.

What next?

Give children a set of sentence frames to prompt their thinking. Can they find the information in the diagram? E.g.:

___'s bar shows that ___.

___ laid ___ fewer/more eggs than ___.

___ and ___ laid ___ eggs altogether.

Going deeper

Ask children to write questions (and answers) which require adding the data from two or more bars, finding differences between bars, doubling or halving amounts, and similar.

T: I'd like you to compare the amount of eggs the chickens laid, and come up with some questions and answers for each other. But I want you to think about these key words: same, double, half, the difference between. And you don't just have to think about two chickens at a time, you can think about more than that. So, for example, which two chickens together laid the same amount of eggs as Yolky?

(Children have time to write their questions and answers.)

C1: Pecky and Dippy laid the same amount of eggs as Yolky when you add them together.

C2: And Roly and Eggy!

T: Good, so together Pecky and Dippy laid the same amount of eggs as Yolky, which is the same amount that Roly and Eggy laid together, too. Well done. Now, what questions have you come up with?

C2: Did Pecky and Dippy lay the same amount of eggs?

T: Good. Did they?

C2: Yes, twelve each.

T: What's another way we could ask that question? If we wanted Pecky and Dippy to be the answer?

C2: Umm ... which chickens both laid twelve eggs?

C1: Or which chickens laid the same?

Notice here how the teacher guides children towards more complex examples.

What makes this statement such a good example of independent, adventurous thinking?

What's the same and what's different about these questions? Is one richer than the other?

Can you extend children's thinking further, by asking them to work backwards from the answer to the question?

T: Good. Any other questions?

C2: Which chicken laid double the amount of eggs as Eggy?

C1: Dippy!

T: Good, how could you ask that question but use the word half instead?

C2: Which chicken laid half the amount of eggs as Dippy?

T: Eggy!

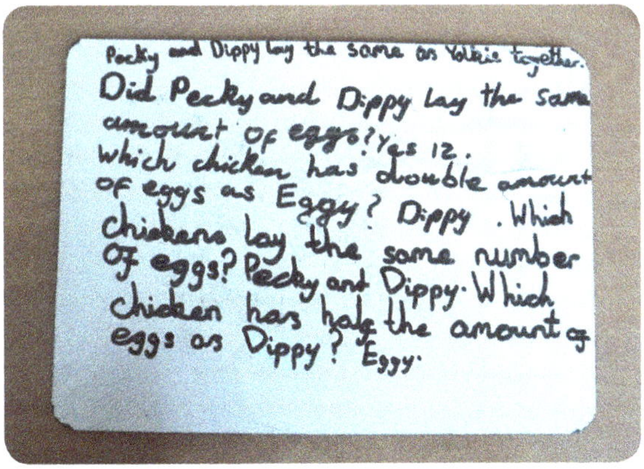

How could you prompt children to demonstrate their understanding of the relationship between doubling and halving in this context?

What next?

If Eggy had laid 4 more eggs, how would the block diagram change? Would the questions still work? How would the answers to the questions change?

Chapter 6
Geometry: properties of shapes

Strand overview

Aims

Children develop fluency in recognizing and naming 3D and 2D shapes, and using properties to classify and sort 3D and 2D shapes and solve problems, e.g. identifying a 'mystery' 3D shape from the 2D impressions or prints made by its faces. Children become fluent using formal mathematical vocabulary as they describe and reason about shapes. They solve problems that develop their understanding of line symmetry: they identify the symmetry, or not, of specific 2D shapes, and they construct symmetrical and non-symmetrical 'whole' shapes from given 'parts'.

Key ideas

- Shapes are a context which support children's developing use of rule-making and generalization, e.g. they recall that every pentagon they have ever seen has had five edges and five vertices, and so they start to generalize that any pentagon they will ever see will also have five edges and five vertices.
- However, children tend to over-generalize, and this can lead to incorrect reasoning, e.g. some children will draw on their prior experience that every square has four sides and assume that any shape with four sides must be a square. Misconceptions such as these should be raised and challenged explicitly.
- Asking children to find, create and draw shapes (e.g. Find a square in this classroom; Draw a hexagon that is symmetrical but not regular) is worthwhile because it is more challenging than recognizing and describing shapes that are presented to them.

Models and apparatus

Constructing 2D and 3D shapes, e.g. using geo strips or straws joined with modelling dough, is important because it requires children to focus on key mathematical properties of the shapes, e.g. To make a cube, how many straws and how many blobs of modelling dough will you need? Constructing shapes in this way makes it easier for children to construct lots of general polygons (not always regular, not always convex) before focusing on specific polygons (in particular, those with conventional names).

View the video on the Year 2 Teacher Support area of the Digital Planner

Progression through the National Curriculum

Year 1

- Recognize and name common 2D and 3D shapes, including:
  - 2D shapes, for example, rectangles (including squares), circles and triangles
  - 3D shapes, for example, cuboids (including cubes), pyramids and spheres.

Year 2

- Identify and describe the properties of 2D shapes, including the number of sides and line symmetry in a vertical line.
- Identify and describe the properties of 3D shapes, including the number of edges, vertices and faces.
- Identify 2D shapes on the surface of 3D shapes, (for example, a circle on a cylinder and a triangle on a pyramid).
- Compare and sort common 2D and 3D shapes and everyday objects.

Year 3

- Draw 2D shapes and make 3D shapes using modelling materials; recognize 3D shapes in different orientations and describe them.
- Identify horizontal and vertical lines and pairs of perpendicular and parallel lines.

Year 2 sub-objectives

Term 2

- Identify and describe the properties of 3D shapes, including the number of edges, vertices and faces.
- Identify and describe the properties of 2D shapes, including the number of edges and line symmetry in a vertical line.
- Identify 2D shapes as the faces of 3D shapes.
- Compare and sort common shapes and everyday objects.

Tasks in Practice

Learning task 5: Mirrors, folding and symmetry

DP Year 2 > Term 2 > Unit 13 > Geometry: properties of shapes > Week 10 > Learning task 5

In this task, children investigate practically the symmetry of 2D shapes.

On track

Children who are 'on track' construct shapes with symmetry and draw (any) lines of symmetry on 2D shapes, rotating the shape if necessary.

This child holds a mirror along the centre of a cut-out irregular quadrilateral.

C: *This doesn't have a line of symmetry, because when you try to do it through the middle, it doesn't show it.*

T: What would you see in the mirror if it was symmetrical?

C: *Equal sides.*

T: You'd see equal sides. What about the other shapes?

C: *The heart has a line of symmetry because when you take the mirror off the middle, it looks the same as the reflection in the mirror.*

(Child holds mirror on centre line of heart shape.)

T: Is there another way you could check if it's symmetrical? Without the mirror?

C: *We could fold it.*

T: Where would you fold it to check if it's symmetrical?

C: *Like this.*

(Child folds the heart in half down the middle.)

T: In half, yes. So what do you notice?

C: *It looks the same on both sides.*

▲ This child uses a mirror to find line of symmetry on heart shape.

What is the value of encouraging more than one way of checking for symmetry?

T: Good language, it looks the same on both sides. Where are you going to draw your line of symmetry?

C: Here.

(Child points to the fold line.)

T: Why there?

C: Because when I folded it, it made a mark.

T: OK, and how does that compare to where you put the mirror?

C: Because when I did it, it was like this (child places the mirror on the fold line) *and it was the same.*

T: Good. Are you going to have a go at drawing it?

You found one line of symmetry on the heart. Is there a different way you could fold it so that it is the same on both sides? Why?

▲ This child is drawing a line of symmetry on heart shape.

What next?

Ask children to draw a shape with a line of symmetry. Ask for an interesting shape, not a square or circle!

Needing support

Look and listen for children who have not yet grasped the reflective property of symmetry. E.g. when folding a parallelogram, they see that the parts do not overlap, but believe that because the two parts are the same shape, the shape must be symmetrical.

The teacher sees that this child has drawn (incorrectly) a line of symmetry on a parallelogram, from one of the parallel sides to the other.

T: Is this a line of symmetry? How can we check?

C: *I can fold it.*

(Child does so.)

T: What do you see?

C: *It folds like a book.*

T: Is it a perfect book? Do the pages match completely?

C: *No. That one's up and that one's down.*

(Child indicates the points that overlap the edges when the shape is folded.)

If this child has only seen some shapes that are symmetrical with lines drawn through the centre, what over-generalization might the child make about any shape with lines drawn through the centre?

T: What can we use to check the line of symmetry?

C: *Use a mirror. I'll put it in the middle, here.*

(Child places a mirror along the fold line.)

T: What do you see?

C: *The shape looks wrong. It's not the same shape in the mirror.*

T: Maybe there's a different line of symmetry. What can you do to explore?

C: *Put the mirror in another place.*

(Child places the mirror along a diagonal.)

T: Does the shape now look right in the mirror?

C: *No.*

T: What would happen if we fold it in half, along that line? Give that a go.

(Child folds shape in half along diagonal.)

T: Is it folding perfectly like a book?

C: *Yes, there's a triangle here and here. They're the same.*

T: But do the triangles fold perfectly together?

C: *No, these bits are sticking out.*

T: So, it's not folding together perfectly. Is this a line of symmetry?

C: *No.*

T: Have we found any lines of symmetry for this shape?

C: *No.*

T: That's right, this shape is not symmetrical.

Why do you think the teacher asked the child to check with a different method?

I have put some shapes that are symmetrical here and some shapes that are not symmetrical here. I have folded them. What do you notice about the shapes in each set? Here are two more shapes I have folded. Which set do they each belong in?

What next?

Ask children if they can write instructions to find and check a line of symmetry.

Going deeper

Ask children to draw this shape on squared paper and then make the shape symmetrical by adding more squares.
Ask children to do so in more than one way.

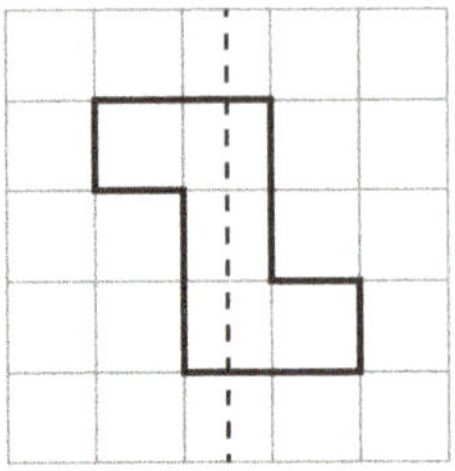

This child is about to start the task.

C: *It has to look the same on both sides.*

T: You're right, it has to look the same on both sides and it doesn't yet, does it? Your challenge is to make it look symmetrical.

(Child places a mirror on the line of symmetry, facing towards the left, and adds a square to the top right.)

T: Is that symmetrical now?

C: *No, the top part is, but the bottom is not the same.*

T: What do you need to do to make the bottom symmetrical?

C: *Put the mirror the other way.*

(Child places the mirror the other way round on the line and adds a square in the bottom left.)

T: Is that symmetrical now?

C: *Yes, because the squares match on both sides.*

The teacher is supporting the child to develop a systematic, iterative approach to problem solving (try, check, refine, check).

T: Exactly, the squares match on each side of the line. Can you draw another one to show me a different way you could make it symmetrical by adding squares?

(Child makes the same drawing and then adds six more squares to create a symmetrical shape.)

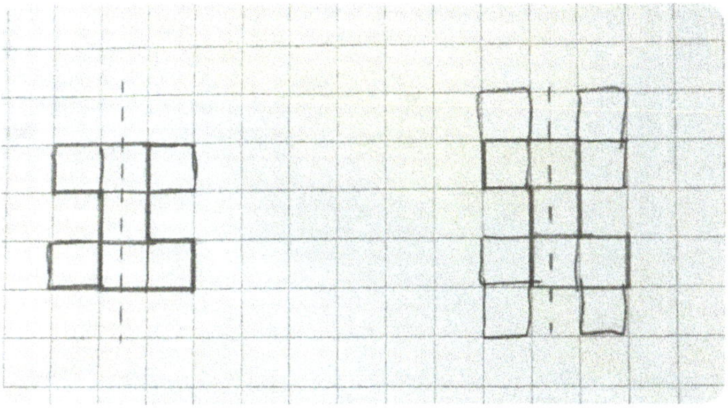

What next?

Tell children we will add some new rules. They can add more squares, but they can also remove existing ones. Each square added or removed counts as one change. They can make up to six changes. How many ways could they make this symmetrical?

Making the shapes with cut-out squares will help children keep track of the changes they have made.

Chapter 7
Measurement

Strand overview

Aims

Children develop their fluency when measuring everyday quantities around them: physical, visible properties such as length, mass and volume; and intangible quantities such as value (money) and time (both 'time now' and 'time from/until/between'). They become fluent with using conventional measuring devices (e.g. rulers, jugs, thermometers and weighing scales), units and scales. They solve problems involving combining, comparing and ordering the numerical values of measurements. They develop their knowledge of the values of standard coins and notes, and use this when reasoning about transactions, e.g. paying a specified amount and then calculating and receiving change. They fluently tell the time to 5 minutes on analogue clocks, and use this skill when solving problems, e.g. placing times in order and estimating and comparing the duration of events.

Key ideas

- Reading a scale is the same as reading a number line.
- Children's familiarity with, and day-to-day use of, money and clocks in their home lives will vary considerably. Determining their prior experience will identify gaps in factual knowledge that can be closed pre-emptively.
- Estimating prior to measuring develops children's familiarity with the size of the standard units.
- Measuring leads naturally to using fractional language, e.g. half full, quarter past 5, spending one-third of my pocket money. In these situations, the equal parts and the whole may not be obvious (e.g. that 5p is $\frac{1}{2}$ of 10p) and so need making explicit.

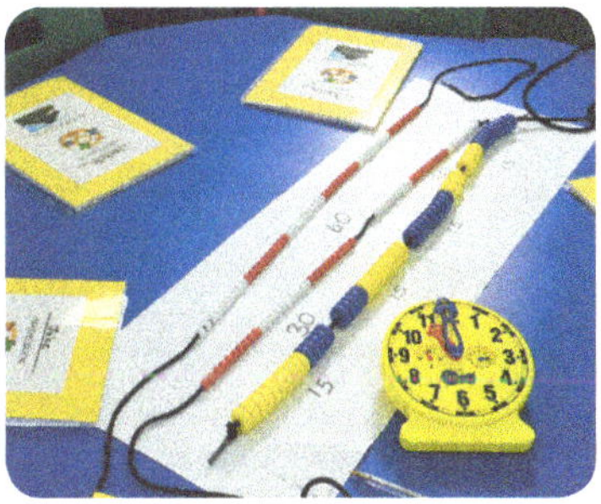

Models and apparatus

Children need to do lots of hands-on, practical measuring to build up their benchmarking of what standard units (e.g. 1 cm, 10 cm, 1 m, 1 g, 100 g, 1 kg, 1 ml, 100 ml, 1 litre) 'look' and 'feel' like, so they can use these as reference measurements, e.g. a forefinger is about 1 cm wide. Children will not develop this awareness if they only read scales.

View the video on the Year 2 Teacher Support area of the Digital Planner

Progression through the National Curriculum

Year 1

- Compare, describe and solve practical problems for:
  - lengths and heights (for example, long/short, longer/shorter, tall/short, double/half]
  - mass/weight (for example, heavy/light, heavier than, lighter than)
  - capacity and volume (for example, full/empty, more than, less than, half, half full, quarter)
  - time (for example, quicker, slower, earlier, later).
- Measure and begin to record the following:
  - lengths and heights
  - mass/weight
  - capacity and volume
  - time (hours, minutes, seconds).
- Recognize and know the value of different denominations of coins and notes.
- Sequence events in chronological order using language (for example, before and after, next, first, today, yesterday, tomorrow, morning, afternoon and evening).
- Recognize and use language relating to dates, including days of the week, weeks, months and years.
- Tell the time to the hour and half past the hour and draw the hands on a clock face to show these times.

Year 2

- Choose and use appropriate standard units to estimate and measure length/height in any direction (m/cm); mass (kg/g); temperature (°C); capacity (litres/ml) to the nearest appropriate unit, using rulers, scales, thermometers and measuring vessels.
- Compare and order lengths, mass, volume/capacity and record the results using >, < and =.
- Recognize and use symbols for pounds (£) and pence (p); combine amounts to make a particular value.
- Find different combinations of coins that equal the same amounts of money.
- Solve simple problems in a practical context involving addition and subtraction of money of the same unit, including giving change.
- Compare and sequence intervals of time.
- Tell and write the time to five minutes, including quarter past/to the hour and draw the hands on a clock face to show these times.
- Know the number of minutes in an hour and the number of hours in a day.

Year 3

- Measure, compare, add and subtract: lengths (m/cm/mm); mass (kg/g); volume/capacity (l/ml).
- Measure the perimeter of simple 2D shapes.
- Add and subtract amounts of money to give change, using both £ and p in practical contexts.

- Tell and write the time from an analogue clock, including using Roman numerals from I to XII, and 12-hour and 24-hour clocks.
- Estimate and read time with increasing accuracy to the nearest minute; record and compare time in terms of seconds, minutes and hours; use vocabulary such as o'clock, a.m./p.m., morning, afternoon, noon and midnight.
- Know the number of seconds in a minute and the number of days in each month, year and leap year.
- Compare durations of events (for example to calculate the time taken by particular events or tasks).

Year 2 sub-objectives

Term 1

- Understand why we need standard units when measuring.
- Read scales to the nearest appropriate unit.
- Compare and order lengths, mass, volume/capacity and record the results using >, < and =.

Term 2

- Recognize and use symbols for pounds (£) and pence (p); combine amounts to make a particular value.
- Find different combinations of coins that equal the same amounts of money.
- Solve simple problems in a practical context involving addition and subtraction of money of the same unit, including giving change.

Term 3

- Compare and sequence intervals of time.
- Tell and write the time to five minutes, including quarter past/to the hour and draw the hands on a clock face to show these times.
- Know the number of minutes in an hour and the number of hours in a day.

Tasks in Practice

Learning task 3: Measuring distance using a metre stick as a benchmark

DP Year 2 > Term 1 > Unit 6 > Measurement > Week 11 > Learning task 3

In this task, children predict and then measure how far a toy car will travel.

On track

Children who are 'on track' begin to estimate length using benchmarks, e.g. I think the blue car travelled more than 1 m.

Three tables are lined up in a row. A small ramp is at one end. Children let a car go down the ramp and leave it where it rolls. It travels to almost the end of the third table.

T: I want you to come up with how far you think the car has travelled. You will be estimating. Think about a metre stick, or a ruler. How long is a ruler?

C: *Thirty centimetres.*

T: Good. How long do you think a table is?

C: *A metre stick.*

T: How many tables long is it here?

(Teacher gestures from the ramp to where the car is.)

C: *Three.*

T: So, how far do you think the car has travelled?

C: *Three metres.*

T: Why did you say three metres?

C: *Because this table is one metre, then the second will be a metre, that makes two metres, and then on the third time that will be three metres.*

T: Yes, brilliant. Because we know that one of these tables is nearly the same length as a metre stick, and so about one metre long, and then another metre for this table and another metre for this table.

> Here the teacher uses the table length as an 'about a metre' benchmark. How will estimation benchmarks for 1 cm, 10 cm and 1 m be thought of in your class?

> *Let's put the cars and ramps in the hall where there are no tables. How are you thinking about estimating metres now?*

On track

Children who are 'on track' measure lengths with a good degree of accuracy.

Three metre sticks have been laid end to end, starting from the bottom of the ramp. The teacher points to the distance a car has travelled beyond the third metre stick.

T: How long are the rulers we usually use in the classroom?

C: *Thirty centimetres.*

T: If you said three hundred here and you add thirty more, how much is that? Tricky question! So we have three hundred and then thirty more.

C: *Three hundred and thirty centimetres.*

T: Good job. Do you want to test your estimate now? Measure to the back wheels of your car. How far is it?

(Children use metre rulers and 30 cm rulers to measure the distance accurately.)

C: *Three metres and twenty-one centimetres.*

◀ This child discovers that 3 table lengths are exactly 3 m and one 30 cm ruler.

▲ Where should the end of the ruler be to make sure you're measuring accurately?

What next?

If the car had travelled half the distance, where would it have travelled to? Can you tell me what the distance would be? Children estimate the new positions of the car and share strategies and answers.

Needing support

Look and listen for children who are not successfully using the metre stick as a benchmark for estimation, and those who attempt to measure using the wrong end of the measuring device or from the beginning of a ruler rather than the beginning of the scale on the ruler.

T: How far do you think the car travelled?

C: *To the middle of the table.*

T: The first table or the second table?

C: *The second.*

T: So you think to the middle of the second table and you've written eighty centimetres?

C: *Yes.*

T: What is it in the classroom that we have been comparing our metre stick to?

C: *Tables.*

T: Well done. So if the car travelled to the middle of the second table, how far do you think it travelled?

C: *More than one.*

T: One what?

C: *One metre.*

T: Good. But not as much as two metres?

C: *No.*

T: Good. Let's measure to check. First, show me ten centimetres on your ruler.

(Children point to 10 cm on the ruler.)

T: Good. Now, can you place a car next to the metre stick to show where it would be if it had travelled ten centimetres?

> 80 cm might feel like a lot for some children. The child here might think that 80 cm is more than 1 metre and is therefore reasonable as an answer. How could we check and resolve something like this?

> The teacher ensures the unit (metre) is included with the number for precision and meaning.

> The teacher is developing the child's estimating skills.

(Children line the back wheels of a car up with 10 cm.)

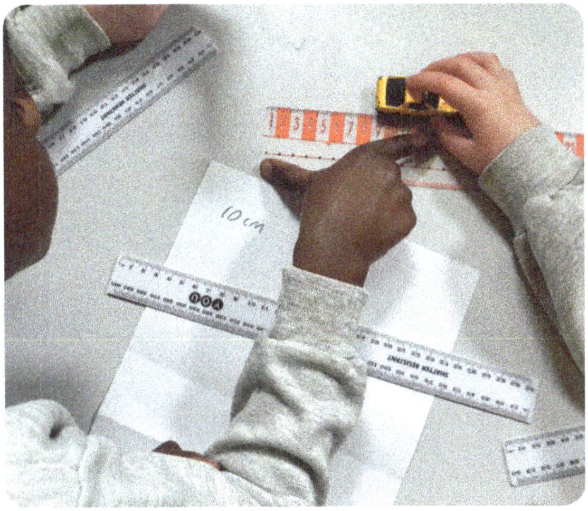

T: Good. Let's count in tens as we measure how far your car went.

(Teacher helps child to measure in steps of 10 cm.)

C: *Ten, twenty, thirty ...*

T: How far has your car travelled?

C: *One hundred and sixty centimetres.*

T: Is it a bit less than one hundred and sixty centimetres?

C: *Yes. We only need to measure up to the back wheels.*

T: How far has it travelled exactly?

C: *One hundred and fifty-seven centimetres.*

T: Brilliant.

▲ The car has travelled one hundred and fifty-seven centimetres.

Here is my car. Can you show me how you would measure how far the car has rolled from the end of the ramp? Check children begin with the beginning of the scale i.e. 0 cm and not the end of the ruler.

What next?

Children find objects about the length of a metre stick. Model the language of a little longer than 1 m, a little shorter than 1 m and about 1 m.

Going deeper

Give children examples of 'car puzzles' such as: The red car travelled 51 cm and the blue car travelled 8 cm further. How far did the blue car travel? Ask children to make up, share with each other, and answer similar car puzzles.

Children position cars on the tables to reflect the numbers in their puzzles.

T: Whose car travelled the shortest distance?

C: Farah's car.

T: How far did it travel?

C: Seventy-four.

T: Seventy-four what?

C: Seventy-four centimetres.

T: Good. Whose car travelled the longest distance?

C: Kyle's car.

T: How far did it travel?

C: Ninety-eight centimetres.

T: How much further is that?

C: Twenty-four centimetres.

T: Excellent. Can you show me? So, starting from the back wheels.

(Child uses a metre stick to accurately measure the distance travelled between the two cars.)

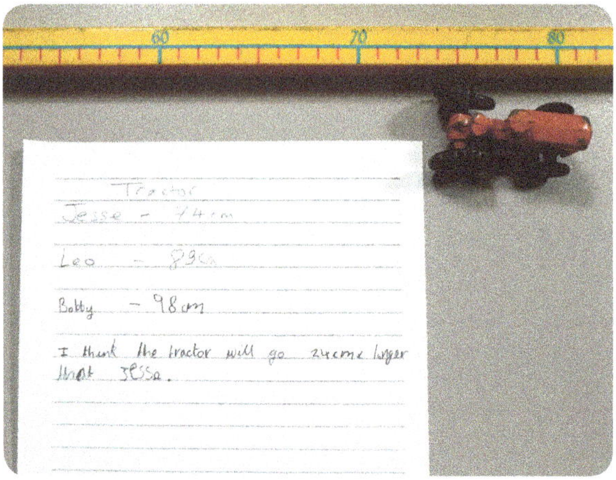

Change the amounts in children's problems by, e.g. 10 cm. E.g. *Farah's car travelled 64 cm. Kyle's car moved 88 cm. How much further did Kyle's car travel than Farah's car?*

What changed and what stayed the same in the two car problems here? Look for children who explain why the difference remains the same: 24 cm. Farah's car and Kyle's car both moved 10 cm less far in the second problem than in the first problem, so the size of the gap between them doesn't change.

▲ How can you make sure you are measuring this accurately?
Can you explain your approach to a friend?

What next?

Children roll two cars down the ramp, one after the other. They write a puzzle using the distances the two cars travelled. They calculate the difference between the two distances, and then measure to check.

Tasks in Practice

Learning task 2: Select coins for a given amount

DP Year 2 > Term 2 > Unit 9 > Measurement > Week 4 > Learning task 2

In this task, children select coin and note combinations to make given amounts.

On track

Children who are 'on track' select coins and notes to pay a given amount, finding more than one way to do this using equivalence. For example, they know that they can pay £15 with three £5 notes or a £10 and a £5 note, reasoning that two £5 notes are equal to the £10 note. Children work out the total of two purchases.

Children are shown some entry prices for a castle. Adult tickets are £5 and child tickets are £2.

T: So, one adult and one child want to visit the castle and we've agreed that's seven pounds. How could they pay for this?

C1: You could use a five pound note and one pound and another one.

T: Does that equal seven pounds?

(Children nod.)

T: How else might we pay for something which is seven pounds?

C2: Erm, two pound ...

T: Are you going to use a two pound coin, or a two pound note?

C2: A two pound coin – there's no two pound note!

T: That's right. What other coins or notes will you use?

C2: And five hundred pennies.

T: So a two pound coin and five hundred pennies. Is everyone happy that this is seven pounds?

Cs: Yes!

Why is the teacher expecting more than one solution?

T: Would I go to a castle with five hundred pennies on me?

Cs: No!

T: Why not?

C1: Too heavy!

C2: And it would take ages for you to get it all out.

T: It would. Are there any other ways of paying for this?

C3: You could have five pound.

T: Five pounds how?

C3: Note. Plus four fifty pences.

T: So, a five pound note plus fifty pence, plus fifty pence, plus fifty pence, plus fifty pence. Can you convince me that that's seven pounds?

C3: Two fifty pence coins is the same as one pound. So four fifty pences is two pounds. Plus the five pounds equals seven.

Would using a number line to represent these different calculations adding up to £7 be helpful?

Have you found all of the ways to make seven pounds using coins and notes?

▲ Recording note and coin combinations for different totals.

What next?

Children work through the different possible combinations of coins systematically for one adult and one child. At first, restrict children to using the high-value coins: £2, £1 and 50p.

Needing support

Look and listen for children whose lack of arithmetical fluency is preventing them from totalling two or more amounts, or who are not familiar enough with the coins and notes and their values, or who mix up the number of people in the problem with the prices of the tickets.

Adult tickets are £5 and child tickets are £2.

T: So we are looking at two adults and three children. How much do you think that is altogether?

C: Thirteen pounds.

T: How did you work that out? You've told me each child's ticket is two pounds.

C: Thirteen pound note?

T: Hmm. Is there a thirteen pound note?

C: Oh. No.

T: Let's write the number sentence for two adults and three children.

(Child writes £6.)

T: Is that everybody?

C: It's two pounds plus two pounds plus two pounds.

T: Is that just for the children? We've got two adults there as well. So, how much is two adults?

C: Five.

T: Is that for one adult, or two?

C: One. So, we need to add another five?

T: Right. So, we are doing five pounds plus five pounds plus two pounds plus two pounds plus two pounds. Let's work it through with a bead string.

(Child and teacher work through the problem with a bead string, sliding across the beads for each person's ticket.)

T: How many beads is that altogether?

C: One, two, three, four ...

T: Pause a moment. How many white beads are there in this group? Don't count them, just tell me.

> Thirteen pounds may be a partially correct answer because this child may have accounted for the two adults to make £10 but then counted 3 children to get £3. How could we find out if their response is a guess, an error of calculation, or partially correct?

> How could assessment and pre-teaching help to familiarize children with coins and notes that do and don't exist?

> Does the child need support because of weak arithmetic skills or because of lack of familiarity with money and money problems?

> The teacher persists with moving the children on from counting in ones.

C: *Ten?*

T: Yes, well remembered. And how many red ones?

C: *Six.*

T: So altogether? Ten and six more makes ...

C: *Sixteen. Ten add six makes sixteen.*

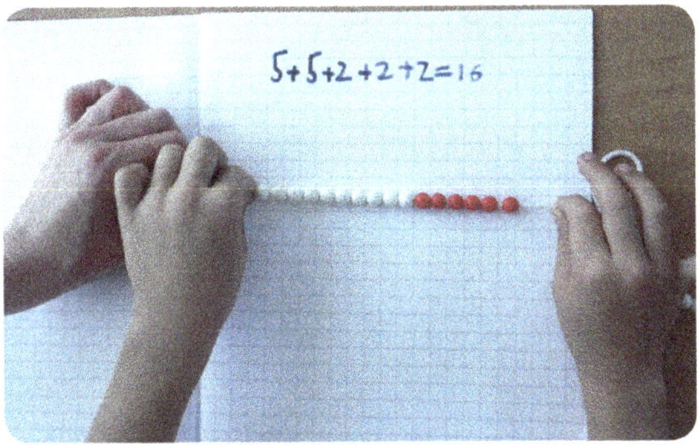

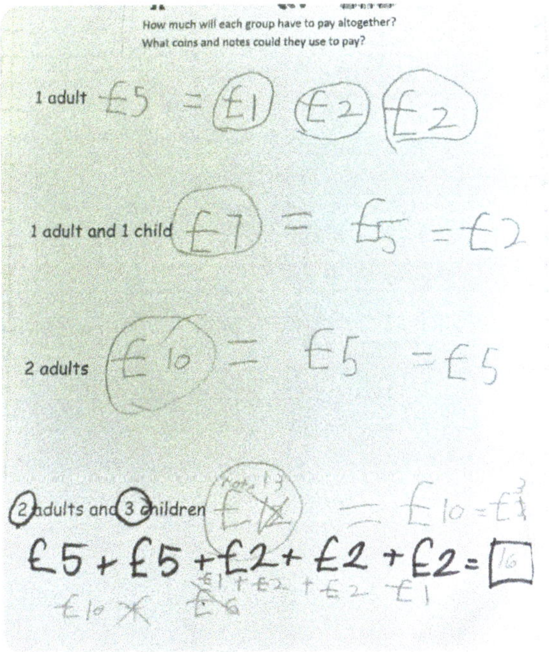

◀ Would drawing 10-frames help the child with the arithmetic?

What next?

Children work through the problems using real, if possible, or plastic money, helping them to remember the shape, look and values of different notes and coins, and also to reinforce which denominations are available.

Going deeper

Provide children specific totals to work from. Ask: *Hassan buys two gifts from the castle gift shop. He pays 68p in total. Which two items did he buy?* Listen to children's reasoning about which objects he could have bought. Some will use estimation to rule out combinations, others will choose pairs of items and either calculate the total or combine the two amounts as actual money and count how much altogether.

The possible items are: pencil 43p, eraser 26p, bouncy ball 25p, postcard 28p, pencil topper 55p, colouring sheet 45p.

Child 1 is one away from the target of 68p. They are looking at the pencil (43p) plus the eraser (26p) which is 69p.

C1: I need one less.

T: If you know that's one pence away from your target number, could you find something that's really close?

C1: So what did I use to work that out? Forty-three pence, the pencil. If I had twenty-five pence that would work. The bouncy ball!

T: How did you know twenty-five pence would work?

C1: Because it's one less than twenty-six pence and I was one away.

T: So which two items is it?

C1: It's the pencil and the bouncy ball.

T: What have you added those two up to equal?

C1: Sixty-eight pence.

T: If I had paid with a one pound coin, how much change would I get? If I paid for those two things? See if you can work that out for me. Think about what you know about how many pennies in a pound.

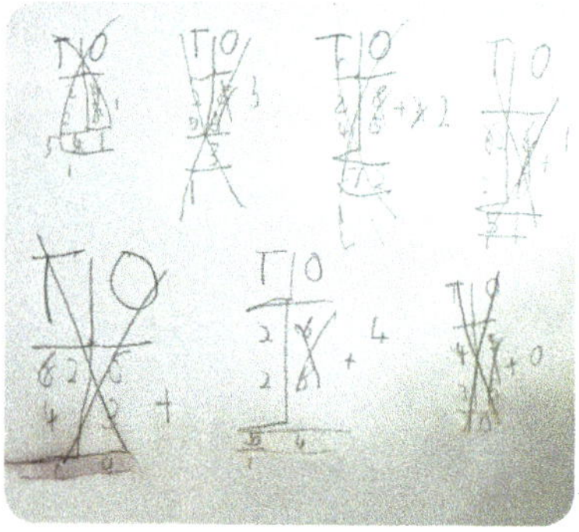

▲ This child is in the process of using trial and error to find the right pair of prices.

If a child is just making lots of 'random' guesses, focus their attention on the ones digits. Ask which combinations can't possibly add up to 68p? Which might?

C1: We'll need a one hundred column.

(Child makes jottings on paper.)

C1: A hundred pence take away ten, ten, ten, ten, one, one.

What common error is shown by this child?

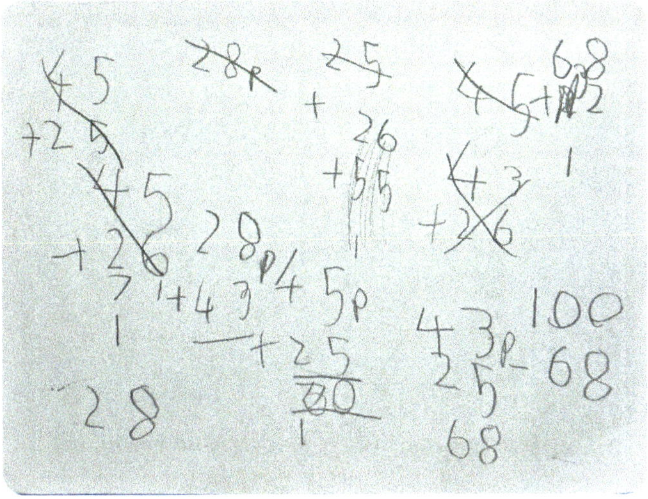

▲ This child has found the right combination and is starting to work out the change from £1.

T: Have we got our change yet?

C1: Ten, twenty, thirty, forty, forty-one. Forty-two pence.

C2: No, you'd get thirty-two pence.

T: Oh, I love a challenge! Agree between yourselves and I'll be back in a moment.

The bead string represents one pound because there are one hundred beads. Here is sixty-eight pence. How many more pennies to seventy pence? How many more ten pences to one pound? How much altogether?

What next?

Children discuss and investigate: one group paid £30 to enter the castle. What combinations of people could be in the group? What combinations of people could it not be and why?

Tasks in Practice

Learning task 3: Halves and quarters on the clock

DP Year 2 > Term 3 > Unit 15 > Measurement > Week 2 > Learning task 3

In this task, children connect half and quarter turns of the minute hand to half and quarter of 60 minutes.

On track

Children who are 'on track' relate 'half past' to the minute hand making half a turn round the clock, from the 12 to the 6.

The teacher holds up a large clock with movable hands. The minute hand is pointing to 12.

T: I'm starting at the top. How many quarter turns is it going to be if I go like this?

(Teacher moves minute hand from o'clock to quarter past.)

C: One.

T: It is one quarter turn, good. It is a quarter of one full turn. Ready? Let's do one more. How many quarter turns is this?

(Teacher moves minute hand to half past.)

Can you show me what one full turn would look like? How many quarters do you think there will there be in a full turn?

◀ The teacher explicitly shows the quarter and half turn and demonstrates that there are two half turns and four quarter turns in a full rotation (one hour).

C: *Two?*

T: It is two quarter turns. Right, I wonder if you can do one for us. Have a go. Start with your minute hand at the top on o'clock.

(Child puts minute hand at the o'clock position.)

T: Don't let anyone see. Move it round and we will work out how many quarter turns you have moved the minute hand.

(Child discretely turns the minute hand from 12 to 6, and shows the clock with the minute hand at half past.)

T: How many quarter turns has he done? He's moved the minute hand from here at the top, down to here. How many quarter turns is that?

C: *Two quarter turns?*

T: It is two quarter turns. What's that the same as? (Pause). Two-quarters, what's that the same as?

C: *A half?*

T: Yes. Do you know how many minutes?

C: *Thirty minutes?*

T: Thirty minutes, good. So two-quarters would be the same as thirty minutes, so half past would be the same as two quarter turns.

What next?

Children work in pairs. Child A moves the minute hand through quarter turns without their partner seeing. Can Child B work out how many quarter turns have been made? How many minutes is it? They start with the minute hand pointing to 12 and then either 3, 6 or 9.

Do I have to have the minute hand beginning at twelve to turn a quarter turn or a half turn?

Needing support

Look and listen for children who don't interchange fluently between units of half or quarter of an hour and the corresponding number of minutes.

Children have bead strings with 60 beads, and have split the beads into two equal groups. One bead represents one minute.

T: We've made two groups of thirty beads, haven't we? I want to break the groups in half again. Show me.

(Child splits the first group of 30 beads into two groups, and the second into three groups.)

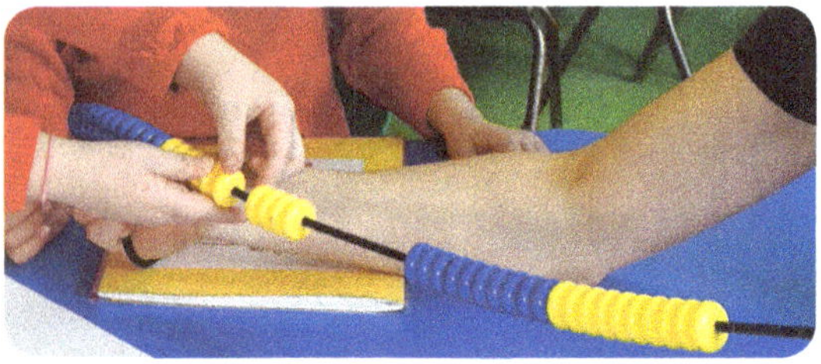

T: Let's look at what you've done. Have you ended up with four equal groups?

C: No.

T: We've ended up with five unequal groups. How could we make four equal groups?

(Child rearranges the first group of 30 beads so they are also split into three groups.)

T: How many groups now?

C: Six.

T: We want four equal groups. Have a look at the clock again. There are sixty minutes in an hour. These sixty minutes are shown on the bead string too. There are two lots of thirty minutes in an hour. (Teacher demonstrates splitting into 2 half hours both on the clock and the bead string.)

T: So, can you show me where we could find four equal parts on the clock?

C: That would be nine and that would be three.

Make the link between a clock and 60 beads on a bead string by using a strip of paper with a paper clip and label marking each 10 minute interval. Lie bead strings next to it for comparison.

How is the child's insecurity with fractions impacting on their progress with finding how many minutes in a quarter of an hour?

Here is the first thirty minutes. Can you show me it in two halves? And again with the second thirty minutes? How many minutes are there in each half? And quarter?

T: The hand could be pointing at nine or three. Let's start with the three then. When it's pointing at the three, how many minutes is that?

C: *Three?*

T: The hand would be pointing to three, but how many minutes is that?

(Teacher shows the bead string again.)

C: *Fifteen?*

T: Fifteen. So many how many do you think might be in each section if I'm splitting into four equal parts?

C: *Three?*

T: Not three ... How many did you just say, how many minutes?

C: *Fifteen?*

T: OK, so how many beads are going to be in the four equal parts?

C: *Fifteen.*

T: Fifteen, yes. What about the rest of them?

C: *Is it fifteen too?*

T: Yes, well done.

How might counting in fives support finding how many minutes in quarter hours and half hours?

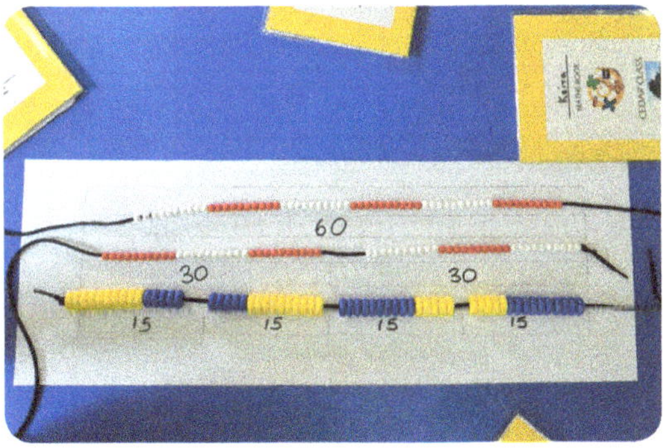

What next?

Children work in pairs. One child represents minutes using concrete apparatus (10-frames, base-ten apparatus or bead strings) and the other shows the same number of minutes on the clockface.

Going deeper

Ask children to fill in the blanks: In 3 hours the minute hand makes:

__ full turns;

__ half turns;

__ quarter turns.

What can you tell me about the turns the hour hand makes in 3 hours?

T: What does a half turn look like?

(Child models a half turn with the minute hand on the clock.)

T: Spot on. How many of those half turns would it do in three hours?

C: *Six. Because it moves two half turns three times.*

T: Well done. Write six down then. Shall we try one more? Shall we try quarter turns? Show me what a quarter turn looks like. What does a quarter turn look like on a clock?

(Child models a quarter turn with the minute hand on the clock.)

T: Fabulous. Show me what three quarter turns would look like on this clock. You've done one quarter, now show me what three-quarters looks like.

C: *So would you go round again?*

T: Would you go round again? Here's one-quarter. Here's two-quarters. So, where would three-quarters be? You've gone fifteen, thirty.

C: *Forty-five.*

(Child points to 9.)

T: Good. So, we've got ... one-quarter, two-quarters, three-quarters, four-quarters. But we say 'whole'. So how many quarter turns in one hour?

C: *Four?*

▲ The teacher shows two quarter turns on the clock, moving the minute hand 15 and then 30 minutes. The child records each block of 15 minutes with base-ten apparatus.

T: Four. You counted one, two, three, four and that's one hour. Can you carry on counting and using the clock to find out how many quarter turns in three hours?

C: *One, two, three, four ...*

(Child points to 3, 6, 9 and 12 on the clock as they count.)

T: So that's one hour...

C: *Five, six, seven, eight ... that's two hours.*

T: Right!

C: *Nine, ten, eleven, twelve. Three hours.*

T: Yes, that's three hours. So how many quarter turns in three hours?

C: *Twelve?*

T: Good. So in three hours the minute hand moves six half turns, twelve quarter turns. What do you notice about the relationship between those numbers?

C: *Double a quarter is half and double six is twelve.*

Pointing to the numbers reinforces the connection between the 'abstract' counting and the 'concrete' quarter-turns.

What supporting resources and questioning enabled the child to be successful?

How will children be supported and encouraged to record their thinking?

◀ How will using base-ten apparatus to represent minutes, help children to describe double and half patterns between parts of an hour? What other resources might they use?

What next?

How many quarter turns in 6 hours? Can you use the number of half turns in 6 hours to help you work this out?

Work with a partner. Ask each other how many half or quarter turns are in 2, 4 and 8 hours. What do you notice? Is there a pattern?

Chapter 8
Geometry: position and direction

Strand overview

Aims

Children develop fluency in describing position, direction and movement. They apply this as they explore patterns and sequences of shapes and objects. They complete patterns, identifying the pattern's physical properties (e.g. it repeats red, blue, green, blue) or geometrical properties (e.g. it repeats triangle, circle, square). They solve problems about direction in practical contexts, such as navigating a partner through an obstacle course.

Key ideas

- Different children will see different patterns in the same sequence, e.g. given a sequence repeating red square, blue circle, some children will express the pattern of the colours, and others the pattern of the shapes. Both are important.
- Patterns can be classified by their structure, e.g. a sequence repeating red square, blue circle, blue square, red circle has an ABBA structure for the colours but an ABAB structure for the shapes. Identifying the underlying pattern of a sequence helps children predict the sections that come before or after the visible portion, and justify their reasoning.
- No pattern can be extrapolated with certainty: the sequence ABCAB... might continue in threes, or fives, or introduce a new symbol D.
- Children should make connections with fractions (quarter and half turns) and measurement (clockwise and anti-clockwise turns).

Models and apparatus

Directing a partner's movement in a large space will help to develop precision of language: the speaker puts themselves in their partner's shoes. They should experience giving instructions that sound different but have the same overall effect (e.g. Quarter-turn clockwise then three steps forward; Three steps to the right then three-quarter turn anticlockwise); and those with a subtly different overall effect (e.g. Half turn then three steps forward; No turn then three steps backwards).

View the video on the Year 2 Teacher Support area of the Digital Planner

Progression through the National Curriculum

Year 1

- Describe position, direction and movement, including whole, half, quarter and three-quarter turns.

Year 2

- Order and arrange combinations of mathematical objects in patterns and sequences.
- Use mathematical vocabulary to describe position, direction and movement, including movement in a straight line and distinguishing between rotation as a turn and in terms of right angles for quarter, half and three-quarter turns (clockwise and anti-clockwise).

Year 3

- Recognize angles as a property of shape or a description of a turn.
- Identify right angles, recognize that two right angles make a half-turn, three make three quarters of a turn and four a complete turn; identify whether angles are greater than or less than a right angle.

Year 2 sub-objectives

Term 3

- Order and arrange combinations of mathematical objects in patterns and sequences.
- Use mathematical vocabulary to describe position, direction and movement in a straight line.
- Use mathematical vocabulary to describe movement, distinguishing between rotation as a turn and in terms of right angles for quarter, half and three-quarter turns (clockwise and anti-clockwise).

Tasks in Practice

Learning task 2: Moving a robot

DP Year 2 > Term 3 > Unit 18 > Geometry: position and direction > Week 5 > Learning task 2

In this task, children use directional language and explore the effects on the route taken by an object.

On track

Children who are 'on track' create one or more sets of instructions to move a 'robot' from one position to another using straight lines and turns.

Child 1 is giving Child 2 instructions to move from one hoop to another, or from a cone to a hoop.

C1: *Quarter turn anti-clockwise. One step forward. Quarter turn clockwise. Three steps forward. Quarter turn clockwise. Two steps forward.*

(Child 2 steps into the hoop. Children record their journey.)

T: Now you need to help your partner to get back. Will the instructions be the same or different?

C1: *Different because it's backwards.*

T: Have a think about it, then see what happens.

C1: *Take two steps forward.*

T: Hang on. Which direction were you facing when you reached the hoop?

C2: *This way.*

(Child points.)

T: Do you need to do something first?

C2: *Turn this way.*

(Child points in the opposite direction.)

C1: *Half turn anti-clockwise or clockwise.*

T: Good. So, write and test the instructions. Think about what's the same and what's different.

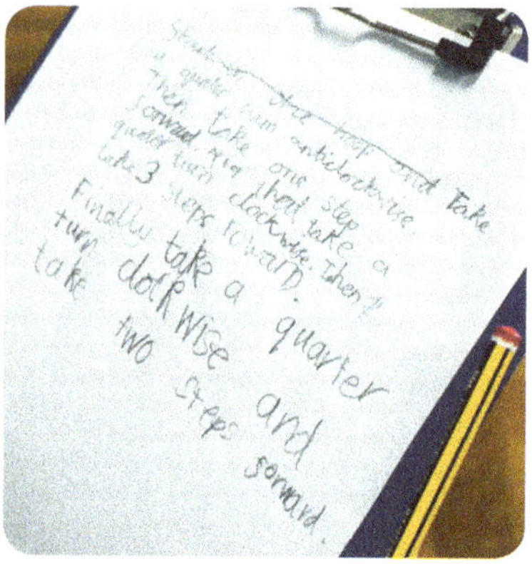

▲ Children record their journey and read it for their 'robot' to follow.

Are children aware that we can turn half a turn in any direction and the result will be the same?

(Children write instructions and then test.)

C1: Half turn anti-clockwise. Two steps forward. Quarter turn anti-clockwise. Three steps forward. Quarter turn anti-clockwise and one step forward!

(Child 2 follows the instructions and steps into the end hoop.)

'Predict and then verify' is a rich prompt for developing deeper thinking.

◀ Can you do the journey in reverse?

(Teacher looks at the two sets of instructions.)

T: So these instructions are going from hoop B to hoop A?

C1: Yes, we did it the opposite way.

T: The opposite way? So, if you did a clockwise turn what would it become?

C2: Anti-clockwise, because we did it in reverse. So, the last turn we did on the way back was anti-clockwise but on the way there it was clockwise.

(Children demonstrate their two journeys, explaining at each turn how it was the opposite to the other journey.)

Did we have to do all of the turns in the opposite direction? Look for children who show you that quarter and three-quarter turns could be done in opposite directions but it doesn't necessarily matter for half turns. Look for children who show you that a quarter turn anti-clockwise will have the same result as a three-quarter turn clockwise.

What next?

Children use programmable robots and give them instructions to follow given pathways, and then to follow pathways of their own choosing around obstacles or to given destinations.

Needing support

Look and listen for children who are not using (or following) left/anti-clockwise and right/clockwise instructions correctly or confidently.

Child 1 is giving Child 2 instructions to move from a cone to a hoop, visiting a second cone on the way.

T: Aisha needs to get to that cone first. What does she need to do?

C1: Anti-clockwise.

T: Anti-clockwise. Are you sure that's what she needs to do first? Remember anti-clockwise is for turning.

C1: No, she needs to go forward first.

T: So, if you want her to move forward, we're going to use the language 'one step forward'. Is that what you'd like her to do? Tell Aisha how much.

C1: One step forward.

(Child 2 takes one step forward.)

T: Now she needs to get to the cone, so she needs to turn. Which way does she need to turn?

C1: Anti-clockwise.

T: Which way is anti-clockwise?

C1: That way.

(Child 1 points clockwise.)

T: Is it? Imagine you're a clock, which way do the clock hands go round?

(Teacher models the clock hands turning with his arms and draws the directions on a flip chart with labels 'clockwise' and 'anti-clockwise'.

C1: Clockwise!

T: Clockwise. OK, how much clockwise? Is she going to do a quarter turn, a half turn, a full turn?

C1: Quarter.

T: Quarter turn. Do a quarter turn clockwise for me?

(Child 1 does a quarter turn clockwise. Child 2 does the same.)

How will children with barriers to processing and following instructions be supported?

Consider providing pictures like logic blocks (e.g. an 'up' arrow to show one step forward, and curved arrows to show quarter turns) that can be stuck onto paper to record the journey.

▲ The teacher models the clock hands turning clockwise and anti-clockwise with his arms.

How could preparing a visual prompt showing direction of turn before the lesson help children with the direction and language of turning?

T: Now what do you want her to do?

C1: One step forward.

T: One step forward, very good.

(Child 2 takes one step forward and reaches the cone.)

T: Now she needs to get to the hoop. What does she need to do now?

C1: Anti-clockwise?

T: Think about the clock face to check.

(Teacher models the clock hands turning with his arms and points to the drawings on the flip chart.)

(Child 2 starts to turn anti-clockwise.)

T: Yes, that's right. Wait. Anti-clockwise how much?

C1: Two steps.

T: Hmm, she needs to do a turn anti-clockwise. What type of turn?

C1: Half turn.

T: Good. Now see if you can carry on.

To what extent is language the barrier for Child 1 here? Look for children who muddle instructions for turn (e.g. right/clockwise) with instructions for travel (e.g. two steps).

What next?

Provide a prompt sheet showing a diagram of the direction of turn and continue to work with children to look at a clock face and reinforce clockwise and anti-clockwise.

Return to the programmable robots and practise simple sequences of instructions.

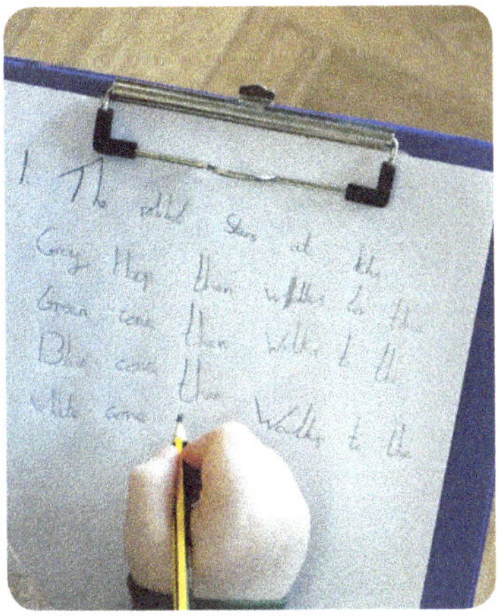

◀ Do you think your instructions will be easy for your partner to follow? How will they know how far to step and which way to turn?

Going deeper

Set up a start and finish point, with two possible routes. Ask children to create instructions for each of the two routes. Which one do they think is easier to follow? Can they explain why?

Teacher has laid out two hoops (the start and finish points), a white cone and a blue cone.

T: Have a look at where the cones are, do you think it will be easier to go past the white cone to the black hoop than it is to go past the blue cone to the black hoop?

C1: I think it would be worse.

C2: I think it will be better.

T: Why? (Pause.) Well let's try. Jack, start in this hoop and let's instruct him past the blue cone to the second hoop. OK, what's the first instruction?

C1: Quarter turn anti-clockwise.

T: Okay, quarter turn anti-clockwise. What's the next instruction?

C2: Move forward two steps.

C1: Move a quarter turn clockwise.

C2: Move forward two steps.

C1: Move a quarter turn clockwise.

C2: Move forward four steps.

C1: Move a quarter turn anti-clockwise.

C2: Step forward two steps.

(Child 3 steps into the hoop.)

T: Brilliant. Now let's look at the other route past the white cone. So, come back to the start. What's the first instruction?

> How does predicting and verifying support children's thinking? Listen to children's reason for their predictions. After verifying, have they changed their thinking? Can they explain why?

> Ask children to record their journeys so they can compare them.

C1: Turn clockwise a quarter turn.

C2: Move forward three steps.

C1: Do a quarter turn anti-clockwise.

C2: Move forward two steps.

C1: Turn clockwise a quarter turn.

C2: Move forward two steps.

(Child 3 steps into the hoop.)

T: Well done! Right, what do you think? Was it easier?

C3: I think going past the white one was easier.

▲ This child reaches the finish point and thinks about which journey was easier.

T: Why do you think that? Look at the cones and the angle they are to the hoops, what do you think?

C1: Because, with the blue one you had to go loads of different ways.

T: Right, so was there more turning or less turning?

C1: Going to the white cone has less turning than going to the blue one.

C2: Yes because that's in a straight line.

T: Do you think that makes the instructions easier to follow?

C3: Yes.

T: Do you agree?

Cs: Yes!

T: Why do you think that is?

C2: Because ...

T: If there's lots of turning there's going to be lots of ...?

C2: Instructions.

T: Yes exactly. So, if there is less turning the instructions are easier? Brilliant, well done.

What's the same and what's different about giving 'moving' instructions and 'turning' instructions?

Should we try to travel in a straight line as much as possible then? Listen for children applying their thinking to familiar routes they take in journeys around the school or when travelling.

What next?

Create some instructions to get from the ___ to the ___ that do not pass next to the ___.

How could you move the robot from ___ to ___ with only three instructions?

Notes